MW00800058

# Searching for Truth with a Broken Flashlight

*-The Reality of Misconception & Wishful Thinking in the Evolution/Creation Controversy*

Michael Hawley

Aventine Press

# Acknowledgments

First, special thanks go out to my manuscript readers. Your expert advice has been invaluable and I am truly grateful. All were handpicked because of their intelligence, judgment, and outstanding literary skills. They are: Bruce Adams, Dave Mercer, Calvin Tanck, Kelly Otto, Joe Whalen, and Jennifer Rastelli. Also, thank you to Phil Carter, Tony Rastelli, Mary Howard, John Looney, Kurt Winter, Tom Schalberg, and Carol Rastelli for assisting me in creating such a valuable resource for those searching for the truth. Nick, Jenn, and Marty, our back porch discussions were so helpful.

I sincerely thank the researchers and scientists in my life that have profoundly affected my way of thinking and that have helped me challenge my biases, regardless of how painful it has been. I especially thank Dr. Rick Batt. Your guidance throughout my graduate experience and exhaustive field research in fossil stratigraphy has given me a strong understanding of objective scientific inquiry.

I am honored to have received spiritual guidance from Pastor Jerry Gillis, Pastor James Andrews, and Fr. Benedict Groeschel. I am humbled by your spiritual wisdom, intelligence, and humility. You are true gifts from God.

Thank you to my mother, brothers, and sisters. You spent years with this stubborn know-it-all and you did not disown me. Finally, I owe so much to my wife, Anita, and to my kids, Brianna, Zack, Jake, Braden, Max, and Tanner. Thank you for being patient with me and reminding me that being a husband and a dad comes first.

# Preface

Christian author James W. Sire defines *worldview* as "a commitment, a fundamental orientation of the heart...which we hold about the basic construction of reality, and that provides the foundation on which we live and move and have our being." For nearly two millennia, devout Christians have had a worldview founded upon Jesus Christ and His Word, the Holy Bible. When a fellow Christian starts out by saying "The Bible says..." the fundamental orientation of their heart is clear, reality is understood through their Christian faith. Around the 18th century, a different worldview began to take hold in Europe and Western society, which has been termed The Age of Enlightenment. Reality is no longer viewed through a biblical foundation, but through human reasoning and understanding. Enlightened thinkers attempted to understand the world logically and rationally, and the culmination of this worldview is modern science. Today, this worldview is alive and well in modern thinking. It is not a big surprise that many Christians and atheists alike consider these two worldviews completely incompatible with each other, and one of the battlegrounds for worldview supremacy has been the evolution/creation controversy. It is my contention that these two worldviews are perfectly compatible with each other, thus, there is no controversy if we honestly believe in God's Providence. Early on, I was blessed with being introduced to the writings of the eminent Christian theologian Thomas Aquinas, who demonstrated how human reason fits beautifully within a Christian worldview. Sadly, his writings seem to have been forgotten or even ignored, and at a time when they are needed the most. The waters of this issue have been muddied by both sides due to misconception and due to a powerful desire for only one worldview to prevail. My book is a reintroduction to one of Aquinas' most persuasive arguments, along with an attempt to clear up the waters.

# Table of Contents

# Chapter 1 – The Quest, a Bicentennial Genesis

*A journey of a thousand miles begins with a single step.*
-Confucius (551 BC – 479 BC)


For many children at the age of four, bath-time was a time of dread, but not for me. It was a time of excitement with re-enactments of ancient predator-prey battles for survival. I had a collection of over fifty plastic dinosaurs that I would line up around the bathtub. Each one would take their turn defeating the bad guy dinosaurs. *Tyrannosaurus rex* was usually the leader of the bad guy dino-gang, but because he was my favorite, *Brontosaurus* won all the battles.

Each member of my family could not help but become a student of dinosaur history. Not only did I enjoy playing with the dinosaurs, but I also loved to learn about them and then give paleontology lessons to everyone I knew, especially to my little sister. When I was in first grade, I recall my little sister's kindergarten teacher confronting my mother and explaining to her how impressed she was that this tiny little girl knew the names of all the dinosaurs they saw during a museum field trip. The thought of this planet being dominated millions of years ago by massive, exotic, and now extinct creatures -before humans even existed- has always intrigued me.

My singular focus upon dinosaurs and other ancient creatures was finally tempered by the time I was a young teenager because of a new interest, astronomy. For Christmas I received a pair of binoculars, with which I began observing the heavens. I was enthralled when I heard how big the Sun actually is, that a million planet Earths can fit inside the Sun. I was then amazed to find out that those tiny stars were also Suns just as big and sometimes bigger than our own Sun. It was mind-boggling to me when I learned that there are more stars in our Milky Way galaxy than there are sand grains on ALL of the beaches of the Earth, and then to discover that there are likewise more galaxies in the universe than those same grains of sand. The astonishment continued when I found out that if a space ship was traveling at 26,000 miles per hour, it would still take it over 100,000 years to travel to the nearest star to our Sun, and it would take over four billion years to travel across our galaxy.

I mention this bit of personal history to demonstrate that natural history and science has always been a passion of mine. Because I was raised Catholic, I had never encountered any conflict between scientific explanations and my faith. The Vatican II Constitution states that scientific theories relating to evolution and an ancient Earth are consistent with Catholic teachings. In fact, it was a Belgian Roman Catholic priest, Monsignor Georges Lemaitre (1894-1966), who first proposed the Big Bang Theory in 1931. I trusted scientists, so I never assumed to question their results. I merely *accepted their conclusions as true*, because they were authorities, or experts, in their field of science.

The challenge to my accepted views about the history of life came in 1976, during the bicentennial of the signing of the Declaration of Independents. The United States was celebrating its 200th birthday. I was in my teens, and I had my first official summer job working for our school district with the custodial staff. One custodian was a devout Baptist, and he introduced me to the young earth creationist belief that everything in the universe was created literally in six days, and that the Earth is about 6,000 to 10,000 years old. He claimed that man and animals were created fully formed leaving no possibility for life to have evolved from a common ancestor. In this young earth scenario, man and dinosaurs coexisted together. He said that before the big flood everything lived to a much older age, so little reptiles grew into huge dinosaurs. Lions, tigers, and bears, lived along side of multi-ton dinosaur predators, such as *T-rex, Allosaurus,* or *Centrosaurus.*

The custodian fervently denied the scientifically accepted claims of an ancient earth and of evolution. It came as a big shock to me, primarily because I had never realized that certain sections of the population did not automatically accept conclusions made by scientists. His counter-arguments against the scientifically accepted history of life and the universe seemed very persuasive, especially since I was completely ignorant of *how* scientists came up the their conclusions, *i.e.,* the scientific process. I just knew *what* they came up with. Additionally, the custodian had creationist literature, which gave his arguments a sense of support and authority.

He then explained to me that scientists did not believe in God, and that their hidden agenda was to take God out of the picture. He believed that there was an academic conspiracy underway to create an anti-God culture, and that scientists are spreading scientific inaccuracies to bamboozle the public.

One particular creationist booklet the custodian gave me had a good looking and well-dressed Christian college student successfully challenging an ugly, deceptive, and ill-tempered science professor during his college science class. The scientist eagerly accepted the challenge, but was then completely befuddled by the student's anti-evolution arguments. I was amazed that the scientist was so ignorant about his own life's work that he had no response to the challenge. This booklet gave the impression that scientific theories dealing with evolution were based upon wild conjecture, and had no basis in fact.

This experience rocked my world. How could my life's passion be nothing but deception? To me, one thing was for sure; one side must be *completely* wrong. I did not want the scientists to be wrong, but then again as a Christian, I did not want to be on the wrong side of God's wishes. It did prompt a question in my mind, however. Why would scientists all over the world dedicate their whole lives to a big lie?

I approached my older sister about my creationist experience. She was in college at the time, so I was hoping that she would have some answers. Her answer was, "Don't make a conclusion until you hear the arguments from the other side, too."

I took my sister's advice to heart, so I began a *quest for truth.* I realized that I had many misconceptions about this issue. I did not know how to best search for truth, but I had an idea. My plan was to not blindly accept either side's arguments as I once did, but to thoroughly evaluate both sides before accepting one as the truth. I wanted to personally discuss scientific theories with actual scientists, and that happened when I got to college.

Once I entered Michigan State University in 1980 as a college freshman, I began searching for any signs of a scientific conspiracy of disinformation. Forewarned is forearmed, so I was prepared to catch them when they slipped up. Even if there was no scientific conspiracy, I wanted to see if scientific theories about natural history were based upon facts or based upon wild conjecture. I was very excited because I was now going to be personally interacting with actual scientists. My undergraduate major was geology and geophysics, so I had ample opportunity to discover whether scientists were purposely being deceptive. In each of my classes, I looked for signs of faulty logic and anti-God deception. Not only did I get to assess all of my geology and paleontology professors, but I also got to assess scientists in other fields. This included astronomy, chemistry, physics, biology, anthropology, social studies, ancient history, and philosophy of science.

By the time I was an upper classman, I had personally conversed with over fifty separate scientists, either individually or in class, from a variety of scientific fields. I purposely questioned them at every turn. I did not find what the custodian and his creationist literature claimed. I saw no anti-God conspiracy within the scientific community, at least at Michigan State. Most professors were actually very considerate of students' faiths, and some were even quite religious themselves.

It was true that they did not mention God in their lessons, but there was a valid reason for that, as explained by my philosophy of science professor. He said that science is merely a tool for understanding nature. Anything supernatural is not testable, therefore, is not useful as a tool to explain things. For example, "How did the 1918 Spanish

Flu kill millions of people?" One could answer the question by saying, "God did it", but that answer will not help us to determine the cause, which could possibly lead to a cure against future killer influenza viruses.

I also did not find any scientific theories based upon wild conjecture. I discovered that scientists are held to strict standards in their research. If their conclusions are not based upon testable facts followed by valid and sound logic, then their research will not get published. The next step is even more rigorous. Once their research is published, then the scientist's peers (fellow experts) in their respective fields review and scrutinize it. Basically, the scientific process is a filtering process to eliminate research based upon conjecture.

I had a chance to practice this peer review for myself during my graduate evolution course work at Buffalo State College. The class was in session every Wednesday night, and the professor would assign one or two recently published science articles on evolution or ecology for the next week's class. We would then spend the full 90 minutes scrutinizing the research. We would answer questions like, "Do you see any possible flaws with the experiment?", "Was the data collected properly?", "Does the data fit the researcher's conclusions?", "Has the researcher taken all of the facts into account?", and "Does the pattern of evidence logically lead to the researcher's conclusion?"

In my opinion, the logic behind the scientific theories that I encountered was strong, but there could still be a possibility of a scientific conspiracy. If they altered the facts before they published their research, then college students like us would never know the difference. The only way to resolve this problem was to do actual scientific research myself, and then compare my results with the results of other scientists. This opportunity came to me with my graduate field research. Under the guidance of my master's research advisor, paleontologist Dr. Rick Batt, I spent four summers doing fieldwork in Western and Central New York. I was tasked to investigate a specific section of Devonian-aged sedimentary rock layers, known as the

Kashong Member of the Hamilton Group. These layers are exposed at certain outcrops in New York State. My fieldwork consisted of measuring and identifying the Kashong sedimentary rock layers and their imbedded fossils. My goal was to determine why the thickness of the twelve Kashong rock layers of shale and limestone at the western sites measured only eighteen inches in thickness, while these same layers at the eastern sites 300 miles away measured over forty feet in thickness.

Rock types indicate the environment in which they formed. For example, shale is basically cemented deep-sea mud, so it indicates a relatively deep-sea environment. When shale particles are put under a microscope they are identical in size, shape, and composition to deep-water sediment mud. Limestone is produced from tropical shallow sea lime mud and corals, like off the coast of the Bahamas today. The limestone and shale layers I was investigating alternate, which suggests a series of sea level rises and falls. Some limestones were very shaley and some shales were very limey, which was consistent with this rising and falling pattern.

In addition to cataloguing the composition and texture of each layer, I also had to collect and identify thousands of fossils within these rock layers. Since sea creatures prefer either shallow waters or deeper waters, the fossils I collected gave me a picture of how deep the waters were. There was a definite pattern to fossils of shallow water creatures found in the limestones and to fossils of deeper water creatures found in shales, which conformed to a slow local depositional process rather than a violent global flood depositional process. The results of my four years of research did not conflict with the scientists' claim of an ancient Earth. To be perfectly honest, my results confirmed their results. It was very interesting to me to see the puzzle-pieces of scientific data fit nicely together. Also, the patterns in the rock layers did not fit with a global flood scenario as claimed by young earth creationists.

So far in my own search for truth, I uncovered neither faulty logic nor conspiracies on the part of the scientific community. Although certain Christians were claiming this, my investigation did not support these accusations. Could it be that the creationists were on the side of error? Might their religious beliefs be getting in the way of sound judgment?

Fate would lead me to the next phase of my *search for truth* of thoroughly evaluating the creationists' side of the issue. I was blessed with marrying into a wonderful evangelical Christian family. Central in their lives is the Bible, faith in Jesus Christ, and the salvation of others. The church we attended (and still do) is a large Christ-centered nondenominational church, called The Chapel. The first thing I noticed about attending The Chapel was that the pastor's messages were always supported by verses in the Bible. To me, his messages were very logical and sound. I had known that a large number within the fundamentalist and evangelical Christian community wholeheartedly endorse the anti-evolution creationist belief, and The Chapel reflected this. My next quest was to discover why so many in this Christian community hate the idea of evolution. I participated in many discussions with many Christians about evolution and an ancient Earth. Some of the discussions got quite heated, but that was not unexpected since this issue hits close to people's religious values. They seemed just as convinced of their views as I was of mine.

This phase of my quest led me to researching in depth the history of the evolution/creation controversy and the validity of creationist arguments. I uncovered numerous misconceptions that if known by today's Christians, might completely change their views upon the issue. Also, I wanted to better understand how the human mind makes the decision to believe or not. Besides misconception, another even larger barrier blocking people's search for truth was wishful thinking. Cognitive neuroscience has advanced significantly in the study of human decision-making in recent years thanks to the use of a technique called functional magnetic resonance imaging (fMRI). How we make decisions about whether to believe or not has a direct bearing upon the path one takes in searching for the truth.

The purpose of a flashlight is to illuminate, or reveal from darkness. This can also be a metaphor in the search for truth. Being absolutely honest with oneself as we seek the truth can illuminate the path to discovery. *Those who are guided by wishful thinking in the face of overwhelming evidence to the contrary are searching for truth with a broken flashlight.* They are searching in darkness. A personal search for truth merely needs honesty and objectivity. Everyone at some point in their life has succumbed to their "wanting" desire for something to be true. Step one is to be open to the possibility that what you believe is true just might not be the truth.

*The search for truth is more precious than its possession.*
-Albert Einstein (1879-1955)

# Chapter 2 - Dual Revelation

*God writes the gospel not in the Bible alone, but on trees and flowers and clouds and stars.* - Martin Luther (1483-1546)


## Roadblocks to Truth: Misconception and Wishful Thinking

In between completing my undergraduate degree in geology/ geophysics and my graduate research in paleontology, I became a commissioned officer and naval aviator in the U.S. Navy for a decade. After a year and a half of military training, academics, officer leadership courses, and flight training, I was assigned to a helicopter squadron at Barbers Point, Hawaii, named HSL-37. My first job assignment (other than flying and looking for submarines) was the squadron legal officer. The legal officer handles all squadron/ command legal issues, including criminal investigations. I attended a legal officer course prior to taking on the position, and the lawyers instructing the course impressed upon us to let the facts speak for themselves when undergoing criminal investigations. They explained that the guilty have a powerful desire to deceive and manipulate, and their goal is to get you to believe they are innocent. They take advantage of people's *misconception* that their intuition is just as powerful of a truth-searching tool as the facts. This misconception is constantly reinforced by exciting fictional detective novels and movies depicting the hero as an unorthodox rogue investigator solving the case by ignoring the overwhelming damaging evidence and following his or her gut instincts. One particular lawyer made the comment that human beings, including highly educated legal officers, have an amazing ability to deny the facts in favor of their intuition. Once you as the legal officer are convinced of their innocence, then you will be a powerful ally in their deceptive agenda to be cleared of all charges.

That year, a sailor had tested positive on a urinalysis test for marijuana use, which is an illegal act in the U.S. military. This prompted me to start an investigation. I followed set legal procedures as required by the Uniform Code of Military Justice (UCMJ) to ensure that the rights of the sailor were not violated. The urine sample's chain of custody was in order, which meant that the sample containing the THC (a result of marijuana burning) came from this particular sailor. Passive inhalation of marijuana generally shows a THC level in a person much lower than 75, such as being present at a party where others were smoking marijuana. This sample had a THC level of over 900, which meant that active inhalation (or consumption) was a virtual certainty.

In this case, the facts were quickly shaping up to a guilty verdict. I was quite convinced that this sailor was guilty. My confidence in his guilt wavered when I began interviewing his workmates, his immediate supervisors, and finally the sailor himself. My first impression of the young sailor was that he was extremely likeable and honest. Tears were flowing down his face as he was denying any drug use. He even "looked" innocent, and my intuition was telling me he was a victim of unusual circumstances where the facts just might convict an innocent man. His personnel record showed that he was an outstanding sailor. All of his immediate supervisors personally vouched for his honesty, moral character, and work ethic. They all believed beyond any doubt that he was completely innocent. Two of his supervisors were close friends of mine, and I trusted their judgment. His fellow workmates echoed the comments made by his supervisors. It was obvious that this sailor was well respected by everyone he came in contact with. I remember feeling that I *wished* him to be innocent. I was beginning to doubt the facts and favor my intuition.

I spoke to my executive officer about my dilemma, and he stated with complete confidence that this young man is "lying through his teeth". My commanding officer agreed with the executive officer, and eventually convicted the sailor of drug use based upon the physical evidence. Since the sailor had such a strong record and contributed greatly to the Navy, my commanding officer agreed to give him a relatively minor consequence, although he still recommended discharge from active service.

Once the sailor was administratively discharged, he came back to my office to sign some paperwork. We had a very cordial relationship, so I asked him, "Now that you are a civilian and there is nothing I can do to you, would you mind telling me the real story?" He said, "Of course I'll tell you. I was lying my butt off! I was bothered that I had to lie to you, but I didn't want to get into trouble." My intuition failed me. He scammed us all (other than the commanding officer and the executive officer), not because he was an evil person, but because he just wanted to be cleared of the charges. He had motive to deceive. My desire for his innocence and my belief in the truth-searching power of intuition made me doubt the overwhelming evidence to the contrary. I learned a valuable lesson.

Because of experiences like these, I became convinced of two things: first, misconception blinds people from the truth, and second, wishful thinking hijacks people's sense of reason and closes their mind to accepting reality. The significance of my Navy experience was that I connected the dangers of misconception and wishful thinking to an entirely different issue, the evolution/creation controversy. As a person with a passion and background in science and as a Christian who embraces the divine inspiration of the Bible, the evolution/creation controversy has always been a constant obsession of mine. Even during my active duty days, I was researching, discussing, and debating people about evolution and creation. I quickly realized that most people, regardless of their educational background, were under the misconception that they had a clear understanding of the controversy. I also realized that their acceptance or rejection of evolution had little to no connection with their knowledge of the evolutionary process.

Every time I listened to arguments on either side of the evolution/ creation controversy one particular H. Jackson Brown, Jr. quote came to mind,

> "The greatest ignorance is to reject something that you know nothing about."

Misconception creates such a smoke and mirrors effect in the search for truth that it diverts one off the path right from the start. Because of this, I will address misconception first, and discuss how it has influenced our ideas, opinions, and beliefs in all areas pertinent to the evolution/creation controversy. In so doing, the veracity of many claims will quickly become apparent. I will then address the issue of wishful thinking and how it has the remarkable ability to effectively close ones mind to the truth. In my opinion, this roadblock is the most damaging, because it obstructs the truth even when one is fully aware of it.

## Nature and Scripture – Misconception within Providence

In divine providence, or "under God's sovereign guidance and control", believers accept that God is omniscient. We also accept that within God's infallible providence he has *revealed* to us truth without error. If true, problems arise not from what has been revealed to us but from our fallible ability to interpret revelation, and this unavoidably leads to human misconception. Inherent in misconception is the power of illusion, because it creates a false sense of reality. It is my contention that misconception through misinformation created the evolution/creation controversy in the first place and continues to perpetuate the controversy. For example, nowhere in the Bible, does it say that one must either believe in God or accept evolution. Much of this either/or misconception lies in the difference between Scripture and the interpretation of Scripture.

Dr. Robert Schneider, professor emeritus of classical languages at Berea College, quotes conservative Baptist theologian Bernard Ramm in his article, *Does the Bible Teach Science?*,

"First, one must realize that revelation is not interpretation, and conversely, interpretation is not revelation. Revelation is the communication of divine truth; interpretation is the effort to understand it. One cannot say: "I believe just exactly what Genesis 1 says and I don't need any theory of reconciliation with science." Such an assertion identifies revelation with interpretation."

Conversely, one must also recognize that evolution, and the scientific process that discovered evolution, does not conflict with a belief in God, as argued by a number of atheists. Science deals strictly with the natural, not the supernatural. To allow research into the supernatural will sabotage the entire scientific process. As I will explain later, this fact is the reason why science is so effective in discovering the realities of nature. Because of this limitation, though, a particular scientist (or anyone for that matter) cannot claim to be an atheist because of the science, such as evolution. If they do, they are basing their disbelief upon a logical fallacy.

A number of Christians have likened the Bible to how Americans view the U.S. Constitution. The U.S. Constitution is the law of the land and most Americans whole-heartedly embrace it, and some even consider it an infallible document. Problems arise in interpretation. Even though it is the law and is considered the accepted truth, we still need the court system to properly interpret it. This is also the case with the Bible. Even though many Christians consider it God's Word, thus, the accepted truth, it still needs to be properly interpreted. When we call upon Scripture as we search for truth, filtering out misconception can only get us closer to the truth.

According to the World Christian Encyclopedia, *there are over thirty thousand different Christian denominations* with a new one forming each week. Members in each denomination believe they have been fully inspired by the Holy Spirit, thus have interpreted the Bible correctly. This means matching interpretation with revelation is a bigger problem than most Christians want to admit. Confidence in a particular interpretation being the truth just might be misplaced. Specific to the creation/evolution controversy, there are multitudes of interpretations of Genesis. There are even dozens of different literal interpretations (not just one as many creationists insinuate to the public) and many of these allow for the reality of both.

Religiously motivated activists often claim that Christians who interpret Genesis with science in mind are dangerously compromising the simplest and most literal interpretation of God's Word. They claim that placing conclusions made by atheistic scientists on the same level as the Bible (or above the Bible) undermines the authority of God's Word. Young earth creationist Ken Ham, president of Answers-in-Genesis, states in his article, *Jesus wrote all of the Bible!* (April 2004):

"...the majority of them [Christian leaders endorsing evolution] have compromised with the idea of millions of years and evolutionary beliefs in astronomy, geology and so on. As a result, the Bible's authority has been undermined through such compromise, and it is thus not understood to be the absolute authority."

Almost all anti-evolution creationists believe that there is a connection between a belief in evolution and the undermining of biblical authority. Notice that a rejection of evolution is not based upon their knowledge of biological evolution and an objective evaluation of evidence, but is based upon this belief. Creationists, such as Ken Ham, do take scientific discoveries into account, but they must be filtered with a favored biblical interpretation.

There are certain groups of Christians that look for truth no further than in the pages of the Bible. These Christians believe that looking in non-biblical sources, such as scientific research; can only cloud the path to absolute truth. It may come as a surprise to some that there are still people living in the United States who believe the Earth is the center of the universe with all celestial objects, including our Sun, orbiting our planet. According to Dr. Donald Simanek, professor of physics at Lock Haven University, these believers fall into two general groups, geocentrists and the flat earthers. Geocentrists believe that the Earth is spherical and is the center of the solar system and of the universe. The daily motions of the Sun, Moon, and stars are the result of the entire universe revolving around the Earth. The modern geocentrist movement can trace its origins in the United States with members of the Lutheran Church, called the Missouri Synod. In 1967, a Canadian schoolmaster, Walter van der Kamp (1913-1998) began the Tychonian Society, and published a journal called the *Bulletin of the Tychonian Society*. In 1984, Gerardus Bouw, an astronomer with a Ph.D. from Case Western Reserve University took over upon van der Kamp's retirement.

The flat earthers not only believe the Earth is the center of the universe, but they also believe the Earth is flat. The modern flat Earth movement can trace its origins to an English inventor, Samuel Rowbotham (1816-1884). He called this geocentric view Zetetic Astronomy, where the Earth is a flat disk centered at the North Pole and bounded on its southern edge by a wall of ice. The Sun, Moon, planets, and stars are only a few hundred miles above the surface of the Earth. John Alexander Dowie, in 1895, established a society in the United States with its central doctrine based upon Rowbotham's Zetetic Astonomy. The organization was then taken over by Wilbur Glenn Voliva, who maintained leadership until his death in 1942. In 1956, Samuel Shenton revived the society's mission, and created the International Flat Earth Society. When Shenton was shown a NASA photo of the Earth in space taken by Apollo astronauts traveling to the Moon he said, "It's easy to see how such a picture could fool the untrained eye." In 1971, Charles K. Johnson became the new president of the Flat Earth Society until he passed away in 2001. Today, the Flat Earth Society maintains a website, which promotes its beliefs.

What both of these organizations have in common is that they base their beliefs entirely upon a restrictive literal interpretation of the Bible. When they argue their beliefs to others they use selected physical evidence, but this evidence is not what they base their belief upon. For most of us, it may seem silly to still believe that the Earth is the center of the universe because of the discoveries made in modern science, but if one bases their belief entirely upon one interpretation of the Bible it can be very convincing. Note the following verses that do more than just hint of the Earth being the center of the universe or it being flat:

-"He has fixed the earth firm, immovable." (1 Chronicles 16:30)
-"Thou hast fixed the earth immovable and firm..." (Psalm 93:1)
-"Thou didst fix the earth on its foundation so that it never can be shaken." (Psalm 104:5)
-"...who made the earth and fashioned it, and himself fixed it fast..." (Isaiah 45:18)
-"And God set them [the Sun and the Moon] IN the firmament of the heaven to give light upon the earth." (Genesis 1:17)
-"...the stars in the sky fell to the earth..." (Revelation 6:13)
-"I saw four angels stationed at the four corners of the earth..." (Revelation 7:1)
-"Fear before him, all the earth: the world also shall be stable, that it be not moved." (Chronicles 16:30)

There are over a hundred verses hinting at an Earth-centered universe. Restrictive literalists, such as Ken Ham, who claim that the Bible promotes a Sun-centered solar system can at best find only a couple of verses that support their argument. Young earth creationists and all other anti-evolution creationists have accepted all of the discoveries made by science, including the Sun-centered model of the solar system, but they deny scientific discoveries made in the historical sciences.

Most creationists recognize that scientific discoveries need to be taken into account, but not at the expense of a favored interpretation. The Bible takes precedence over the science. Only then can we be confident the Holy Spirit has inspired our reasoning. According to this way of thinking, the spiritually safe approach is to filter science with the Bible. Cofounder of modern flood geology and creation science, Henry Morris, puts it this way:

"It is not only legitimate then, but absolutely mandatory, for the Christian to depend implicitly on the scientific and philosophic framework revealed in Holy Scripture if he is to attain a true understanding of any of the factual data with which science deals, and their implications."

The danger to this approach is that we must assume a favored interpretation of Genesis is the absolute truth. There are many literal interpretations of Genesis, and the flat earthers have taken the simplest and most literal one. Biblical interpretation has a history of human error. As stated earlier, the fact that there are over 30,000 different Christian denominations is a testament to the difficulties in biblical interpretation. This means that using the Bible as the primary source in understanding nature *introduces human error*.

Augustine of Hippo (354-430) was the most influential Christian theologian up until the Early Middle Ages. Augustine warned Christians seventeen hundred years ago against denying discoveries made in science merely because they contradicted a favored literal biblical interpretation. He states in his work, *On the Literal Meaning of Genesis*,

"Usually, even a non-Christian knows something about the earth, the heavens, and the other elements of this world, ...and so forth, and this knowledge he holds to as being certain from reason and experience. Now, it is a disgraceful and dangerous thing for an infidel to hear a Christian, presumably giving the meaning of Holy Scripture, talking nonsense on these topics; and we should take all means to prevent such an embarrassing situation, in which people show up vast ignorance in a Christian and laugh it to scorn. The shame is not so much that an ignorant individual is derided, but that people outside the household of the faith think our sacred writers held such opinions, and, to the great loss of those for whose salvation we toil, the writers of our Scripture are criticized and rejected as unlearned men.... Reckless and incompetent expounders of Holy Scripture bring untold trouble and sorrow on their wiser brethren when they are caught in one of their mischievous false opinions and are taken to task by these who are not bound by the authority of our sacred books. For then, to defend their utterly foolish and obviously untrue statements, they *will try to call upon Holy Scripture for proof* and even recite from memory many passages which they think support their position, although they understand neither what they say nor the things about which they make assertion."

Fifteen hundred years later, Princeton evangelical theologian and champion of biblical inerrancy, Charles Hodge (1797-1878), gave a similar warning to fellow believers,

"...theologians should not ignore the teachings of science... it is unwise for theologians to insist on an interpretation of Scripture which brings it into collision with the facts of science."

Anti-evolution creationists are faced with an undeniable fact; the scientific community of experts considers biological evolution a reality (both establish theory and fact). It seems that the anti-evolution claim is an excellent example of what Augustine and Hodge were warning about, since it collides directly with the facts of science. The practice of evaluating Scripture to filter out the correct literal interpretation of Genesis has not produced agreement among creationists.

A Christian friend of mine replied to me after I had explained to him some of the biblical proofs for an ancient earth, "Well, we can agree to disagree. You can believe in the interpretation you want and I can believe in the interpretation I want." If this is the case, then one of us is settling upon believing in something that is absolutely wrong. It also suggests that searching for truth about nature (as in the origins of the universe and of life) by primarily interpreting Scripture has an inherent limit and has no way of confirming ones beliefs.

Modern science has a rigorous self-correcting process, which is designed to filter out incorrect scientific interpretations, *i.e.*, human error. The advances in science and technology in the last hundred years is a testament to the effectiveness of this process. Interpreting the Bible is at the mercy of a fallible interpreter's thinking. If there was another infallible divine source, *i.e.*, a source of absolute truth, then we could evaluate every literal interpretation of the Bible with it and filter out the bad ones. The remaining interpretation would most likely be the truth. Is there another infallible source? The answer is, yes, and it is *God's other infallible revelation, nature itself.* This should be ideal for issues that involve both the Bible and nature.

According to the Bible, God's revelation does not begin and end with just the Scripture. Notice what the apostle John says in chapter 21, verse 25:

"And there are also many other things which Jesus did, the which, if they should be written every one, I suppose that even the world itself could not contain the books that should be written. Amen." (KJV)

So, the Bible does not contain God's complete revelation. It may be sufficient for our path to salvation, but it does not contain everything. Paul explains that we must look in the physical world to help us further understand his revelation:

"The invisible things of God are understood by the things that are made." (Romans 1:20 KJV)

Is the Bible silent on what "the things that are made" is? No. The Bible does identify another source of his revelation in Psalm 19:1:

-"The heavens declare the glory of God; and the firmament showeth his handywork." (KJV)

Nature is the other source of revelation. If nature is God's work, then it must be infallible. Regardless of the context of Psalm 19:1, it reveals that the heavens, i.e., everything in nature, are another source of absolute truth. Since Christians believe that the Bible is God's Word and nature is God's handiwork, then there should be perfect harmony between the two. All we need to do is compare the two. If two of the interpretations are not in harmony, then one or both of the interpretations must be wrong. If two are in harmony, then we may have found the truth.

There is a possible reason why religious leaders do not explain to their followers this point. *To a hammer, everything looks like a nail.* To a theologian endlessly studying the Bible, absolute truths are only found in Scripture. Some claim that God's Word is completely sufficient, as explained in 2 Timothy 3:16. This verse does say that Scripture is sufficient, but for the purpose of salvation not for the purpose of understanding nature.

Harmonizing God's infallible Word with God's infallible handiwork can be considered a dual revelation approach in order to better discover the absolute truth about God's Word. This approach is not new. Thomas Aquinas (1225-1274) argued this approach nearly eight hundred years ago. Thomas Aquinas is considered by historians to be one of the most influential European theologians and philosophers of the Middle Ages. Almost single-handedly, he shifted medieval philosophy away from Plato and towards Aristotle. He believed human reason was used in theology not to prove the truths of faith, but to defend it, and one way was with dual revelation. He called the Bible *special revelation* and he called nature *general revelation*. He believed this approach helped clarify Scripture, and he also believed the early scientists (he called them natural philosophers) were revealing truth about nature. Aquinas states in *Summa Theologiae* (1273):

"...the philosophical doctrines [natural laws] which can be investigated by reason, there be a sacred doctrine known through revelation...Nevertheless, sacred doctrine also used human reason. It does so not to prove the faith – for that would detract from the merit of faith – *but to clarify some of its implications.* Therefore, since grace protects nature rather than erasing it, natural reason should serve faith just as the natural inclination of the will obeys love.... The apostle Paul speaks of "bringing every understanding into captivity in the service of Christ" (II Cor 10:5). Thus sacred doctrine appeals to the authority of philosophers [scientists] *in those areas* where they were able to arrive at the truth through natural reason..."

Dr. Schneider quotes Sir Francis Bacon (1561-1626), Lord Chancellor to King James I, the same man whose name appears on the King James Bible,

"Let no man...think or maintain that a man can search too far or be too studied in the book of God's Word or in the book of God's Works, divinity or [natural] philosophy."

Notice how similar the paths of theologians and scientists are from a Christian perspective. Theologians study God's infallible Word, while scientists study God's infallible Work. Biblical verses are puzzle pieces for theologians to discover the mysteries of the Bible, just as facts in nature are puzzle pieces for scientists to discover the mysteries of nature. To not put physical evidence on equal footing with biblical verses in interpreting nature is to not fairly accept all of God's infallible revelations. As a Christian, if we study both infallible gifts properly, it can be argued that we have a greater potential for success in discovering the truth.

Creationist Marvin Lubenow does not agree with Thomas Aquinas that God's revelation can be clarified by His handiwork. In his book, *Bones of Contention* (1992), he writes:

"[Dual Revelation is] foolishness because of the nature of biblical truth in contrast to the nature of scientific truth. Whether one agrees with it or not, the Bible claims to be truth in the absolute sense, including its statements about nature. On the other hand, philosophers of science are unanimous in recognizing that science does not-in fact, cannot-traffic in absolute truth. All scientific truth is relative. What strange twist of logic would cause us to think that absolute truth and relative truth can be or should be harmonized?" (p.245/246)

Lubenow has made a fatal error. He has created an invalid argument, because it is based upon flawed logic. He has confused nature with science. Science is merely the study of nature. Because nature is God's creation, it is an absolute truth just as the Bible is. Science is merely man attempting to discover nature's absolute truths using a less dogmatic approach in order to avoid *absolute error*. Lubenow is stuck on the process of science, which is neither of the infallible revelations.

When someone attempts to explain nature with a favored biblical interpretation, like biblical proof of a global flood, he is not using all sources of absolute truth. Why not read clues in nature to understand nature, since it is also absolute truth? Reading only half of the story thanks to being bound to a specific interpretation only gets one half way there. Knowing that the process of biblical interpretation is wrought with human fallibility, it is only logical to weigh in ALL of the evidence.

There are a number of advantages God's handiwork (nature) has over God's Word as it relates to interpreting nature. First, the primary purpose of God's Word is something other than interpreting nature. This increases the difficulty in deciphering the riddles of nature, which increases the potential for human error in interpretation. Second, the great thing about nature is that we can guarantee humans did not make any dictation or translations mistakes, as they have as they co-authored today's Bibles. Human beings are directly interpreting an absolute truth. There are no translation errors in nature. Third, as Bible believing Christians, we believe in biblical inerrancy, but this is an assumption on our part. There is no way of proving it. There IS no assumption about nature's inerrancy. *Convincing an atheist or a Muslim that the Christian Bible is inerrant and infallible is a difficult task, although convincing them that nature has not been tainted by human fallibility has few roadblocks.*

If we are to discover the truths about nature, and we have the two divine revelations at our disposal, which revelation should we interpret first now that we know scriptural infallibility and inerrancy requires another level of interpretation (possible chance of error) that nature does not? My contention is to let the facts of nature fall where they fall, *i.e.,* let the truth reveal itself. Only then do we use the Bible in interpreting natural events. If we honestly believe in the infallibility and inerrancy of the Bible, then the facts of nature will automatically conform to the correct interpretation. If we use this method, then we have not introduced potential biblical interpretation errors. Jewish tradition has supported this approach. Rabbi Saadia Gaon of Babylonia (882-942) argued that the Bible should never be interpreted contrary to senses or reason. Rabbi Jeffrey Tigay points out that Abraham Isaac Kook (1865-1935), unquestionably one of the most celebrated and influential Jewish Rabbi's of the 20th century,

"...held that scientific ideas which seem to conflict with the Torah need not necessarily be opposed, but can serve as stimuli to delve more deeply into the Torah and discover more profound meaning in it."

# Chapter 3 – In the Beginning

*When I want to understand what is happening today or try
to decide what will happen tomorrow, I look back.*
-Oliver Wendell Holmes, Jr. (1841-1935)

## Historical Misinformation

As I discussed and debated issues about the evolution/creation
controversy, it became apparent that many misconceptions were the
result of historical misinformation. For example, both pro- and anti-
evolutionists have settled upon the idea that today's controversy can
be traced back to Galileo Galilei (1564 – 1642) and his confrontation
with the Catholic Church in 1632. This is simply not the case, as I
will explain in this chapter. Incidentally, it is also a misconception
that the Catholic Church imprisoned Galileo because he rejected the
Ptolemaic model (Earth centered universe), insinuating that the Church
feared the progress of science. Although the Catholic Church, as well
as all Protestant denominations at that time, continued to promote
the Ptolemaic model and the Church officially forbade Galileo to
publically promote the Copernican model (Sun centered solar system)
as the truth, they approached it *donec corrigatur*, which means
"forbidden until corrected". They were open to the possibility of
the Copernican model, but only until it was finally accepted by the
experts. The problem was in 1632 many experts still rejected the Sun
being the center of the solar system, and full acceptance did not occur
until 1857. The issue for the Church was that Galileo rejected their
authority by publically promoting it.

I will be addressing a number of other misconceptions caused by
historical misinformation, and I believe the most damaging of these
was a dirty little secret held by Henry Morris, founder of modern

creation science. Unknown to all modern day creationists is the fact that the one and only proof of a global flood, all layered sedimentary rocks, can be traced directly to a dream of a teenager in the nineteenth century who claimed it was a vision from God.

## The Driving Force behind the Evolution/Creation Controversy

Recent polls indicate that the majority of Americans believe biological evolution conflicts with their faith and they do not believe biological evolution had a role in the origin of human beings (USA Today/Gallup 2007: 47-66%, Newsweek 2007: 48%, Gallup 2006: 46%, CBS 2006: 53%, CNN/USA/Gallup 2005: 53%, Harris 2005: 54%, NBC 2005: 57%). In stark contrast, the experts overwhelmingly accept that human beings and all other organisms evolved from an ancient common ancestor (National Science Foundation 1999: 99.95%). Millions of Americans have made a conscious decision to ignore the conclusions made by the experts in favor of what they believe their religious authorities have concluded. Interestingly, the majority of these Christians are unaware of what their own religious denomination has endorsed. According to Molleen Matsumura of the National Center for Science Education, of the twelve major Christian denominations, at least 77% belong to churches that support the reality of biological evolution. These groups include the Roman Catholic Church and most mainline Protestant denominations, such as The United Methodist Church, National Baptist Convention of America, Evangelical Lutheran Churn in America, Presbyterian Church (USA), African Methodist Episcopal Church, the Episcopal Church, and others. This means tens of millions of Christians in America have a misconception about their own denomination's stand on the evolution/ creation controversy.

One probable reason why so many Christians have this misconception is because their information/education came from a source other than their own religious leaders. Anti-evolution literature is readily available in most bookstores and on the internet. Anti-evolution creationists are relentless in getting their information out to the public. For example, February 12, 2009, was Charles Darwin's 200th birthday. In order to best exploit any potential renewed interest in Darwin, anti-evolution creationists made available an attractive reprint of his famous work, *On the Origins of Species*, for all of the bookstores. Unbeknownst to the buyer, this reprint is filled with anti-evolution information that Charles Darwin would completely reject. The time, energy, and financial resources backing a project of this magnitude demonstrate the zeal behind these creationists. It is not a stretch of logic to see why the public receives much of its education about biological evolution from anti-evolution literature.

Identifying anti-evolution groups may reveal the driving force behind the evolution/creation controversy. Why focus upon anti-evolution groups? The scientific community is not the driving force behind today's evolution/creation controversy. Scientists use professional scientific journals as their venue to communicate information, but these journals are silent about the controversy. They focus strictly upon the science behind evolutionary theory. In other words, while anti-evolution creationists produce anti-evolution literature, the scientific community does not produce anti-creation literature. The Jewish community is not the driving force behind the controversy. The modern-day Orthodox Jewish view sees no conflict between discoveries made in science and the Bible, which includes biological evolution, an ancient universe, and a local Noachian flood. The Rabbinical Council of America (RCA) has stated that a proper understanding of evolutionary theory is compatible with belief in a Divine Creator and with the first two chapters of Genesis. The modern-day Conservative Jewish View also believes science is a tool to learn about God's creation yet has not made an official response to evolution. Most see no conflict as long as it is considered God's handiwork.

The following are a number of notable anti-evolution groups: the *Creation Research Society,* the *Institute for Creation Research,* the *Discovery Institute, Answers-in-Genesis, Center for Scientific Creationism, Creation Evidences Museum,* and *Reasons to Believe.* If one investigates a more complete collection of anti-evolution groups, it will be apparent that these particular groups do an excellent job of representing their beliefs. Comparing the similarities of these groups reveals a pattern, which in my opinion identifies the driving force behind the modern evolution/creation controversy. With few exceptions, all of these organizations belong to the conservative evangelical and/or fundamentalist section of the Christian community. Conservative evangelical and fundamentalist Christians, make up only 15-20% of the American Christian population, and a 2005 Pew Research Center poll has found that the vast majority (over 70 percent) of these Christians do not believe evolution had any part in the origins of man. Understanding why this section of the Christian community is so relentless in getting their anti-evolution beliefs out to the public may be found in how they distinguish themselves from other Christians. British historian David Bebbington, in his study of evangelism in Great Britain, discovered four common characteristics of evangelicals. They are:

1. *Conversionism* – Emphasis on the conversion experience, also called being saved, or being born again.
2. *Biblicism* – The primary or sole source of religious authority is the Bible. Bible prophecy is often emphasized.
3. *Crucicentrism* – A central focus on Christ's redeeming work on the cross as the only means for salvation and the forgiveness of sins.
4. *Activism* – Encouragement of evangelism, or sharing one's beliefs.

To evangelicals, activism is a divine directive. "Go ye, and make disciples of all nations in my name." (Matthew 28:19) To many, the word "fundamentalist" is synonymous with the word "evangelical" but this is only partially correct. There is a slight distinction. Fundamentalist Christians also adhere to these characteristics, thus, fit under an overarching term of evangelical, but tend to be on the conservative end of the evangelical spectrum. Fundamentalists are more dogmatic in their doctrinal beliefs, i.e., the fundamentals. This promotes a practice of exclusion with the fundamentalists, where they openly criticize others for their beliefs. For example, when the citizens of Dover, Pennsylvania, voted the intelligent design anti-evolution creationists off the school board in November 2005, conservative televangelist Pat Robertson publically stated on his show, *The 700 Club,* "I'd like to say to the good citizens of Dover: if there is a disaster in your area, don't turn to God -- you just rejected Him from your city,"

Most evangelicals tend to be more open to differing interpretations of the Bible, as long as it does not conflict with the four common characteristics. Churches that see no conflict between biological evolution and faith are beginning to recognize that their parishioners have been influenced by anti-evolution material, and they are finally responding. For example, in 2004 school officials in Grantsburg, Wisconsin, created a policy requiring the students to be able to explain "the scientific strengths and weaknesses of evolutionary theory". This policy change is a common technique employed by anti-evolution groups for the purpose of getting their material into the public science classroom. The policy prompted a signed letter by 188 pastors and priests in Wisconsin from Baptist, Catholic, Episcopal, Lutheran, Methodist and other Christian denominations supporting evolutionary theory and rejecting the religious anti-evolution agenda. The following is their letter.

"Within the community of Christian believers there are areas of dispute and disagreement, including the proper way to interpret Holy Scripture. While virtually all Christians take the Bible seriously and hold it to be authoritative in matters of faith and practice, the overwhelming majority do not read the Bible literally, as they would a science textbook. Many of the beloved stories found in the Bible – the Creation, Adam and Eve, Noah and the ark – convey timeless truths about God, human beings, and the proper relationship between Creator and creation expressed in the only form capable of transmitting these truths from generation to generation. Religious truth is of a different order from scientific truth. Its purpose is not to convey information but to transform hearts.

We the undersigned, Christian clergy from many different traditions, believe that the timeless truths of the Bible and the discoveries of modern science may comfortably coexist. We believe that the theory of evolution is a foundational scientific truth, one that has stood up to rigorous scrutiny and upon which much of human knowledge and achievement rest. To reject this truth or to treat it as 'one theory among others' is to deliberately embrace scientific ignorance and transmit such ignorance to our children. We believe that among God's good gifts are human minds capable of critical thought and that the failure to fully employ this gift is a rejection of the will of our Creator. To argue that God's loving plan of salvation for humanity precludes the full employment of the God-given faculty of reason is to attempt to limit God, an act of hubris. We urge school board members to preserve the integrity of the science curriculum by affirming the teaching of the theory of evolution as a core component of human knowledge. We ask that science remain science and that religion remain religion, two very different, but complementary, forms of truth."

## The Origin and Evolution of the Modern Evolution/Creation Controversy

### *Sola Scriptura* and Restrictive Literalism

Anti-evolution creationists have either correctly embraced the truth, which means that the scientific experts got it all wrong, or they have inadvertently embraced falsehood. Understanding the reason why they are so vehemently against biological evolution will further clarify the controversy, and in so doing, get us one step closer to the truth. This search must begin with an examination of the evolution/creation controversy's beginnings and how it has evolved into what we see today. Because the driving force behind the controversy is the fundamentalist/evangelical branch of the Protestant community its origins will be found within Protestant history, especially in their method of biblical interpretation. Prior to this, the only Christian church in Western Europe was the Catholic Church, and dogmatically accepting only one literal interpretation of Genesis, *i.e.,* a restrictive literal interpretation, as it relates to natural events was not the general practice. Although Catholic theologians interpreted Scripture literally, a restrictive literal interpretation approach was of little importance. The Church followed the lead of theologian Augustine of Hippo (354-430). He was the primary influence upon the minds of clergy up until the Early Middle Ages. Augustine states in his work, *On the Literal Meaning of Genesis*,

"...in interpreting words [in the Book of Genesis] that have been written obscurely for the purpose of stimulating our thought, I have not rashly taken my stand on one side against a rival interpretation which might possibly be better."

As stated earlier, Augustine warned of being too restrictive in interpreting Scripture, especially when it deals with nature.

Incidentally, Augustine did not take the most literal interpretation of Genesis 1 and Genesis 2. He states,

"These seven days of our time, although like the same days of creation in name and in numbering, follow one another in succession and mark off the division of time, but those first six days occurred in a form unfamiliar to us as intrinsic principles within things created…disposing them [days] in an order not on intervals of time but on causal connections."

The general practice of literally interpreting the Book of Genesis in a restrictive manner began with Martin Luther and the Protestant Reformation. In 1517, Martin Luther (1483-1546) nailed his 95 Theses of Contention to the Wittenberg Church door in a demonstration of protest to what he believed were corrupt religious practices within the Roman Catholic Church. In just weeks, copies of his 95 theses were posted in almost every German town. This act suddenly caught the interest of millions of people. Two years later, Luther experienced a moment of enlightenment in the Wittenberg Tower giving rise to the doctrine of *Sola Fide* (salvation by faith alone), the cornerstone guiding principle for many fundamental and evangelical Protestant Christians. He discussed this conversion experience in a later work: "I began to understand that this verse means that the justice of God is revealed through the Gospel, but it is a passive justice, i.e., that by which the merciful God justifies us by faith, as it is written: "The just person lives by faith." All at once I felt that I had been *born again* and entered into paradise itself through open gates."

In 1521, Luther proclaimed at his trial that religious authority lay not with the Pope, but with Scripture itself. Thus began the Protestant Reformation and its central theological doctrine of *Sola Scriptura*, which means religious authority rests solely in Scripture and not with religious leaders. Warfare, plagues, poverty, and corruption created a Europe ripe for a grassroots religious movement against the established authority. Luther quickly found support and protection from local noblemen believing in his cause, which allowed him to advance his theology, later to be called Lutheranism. Luther's separation also paved the way for other local European communities to follow suit who were equally unhappy with the religious establishment. Learned religious reformers familiar with Scripture soon realized that the guiding principle of *Sola Scriptura* allowed them a choice to fully embrace Lutheranism or to follow their own biblical interpretations, depending upon what they believed the Holy Spirit was telling them. These kinds of theological disagreements between reformers created numerous Protestant groups, and one of the earliest to form was the Anabaptists. Christoph Fischer, a Catholic priest at Feldsberg, Austria, wrote in 1615 about the connection between Luther and the Anabaptists. He stated, "Among all the heretical sects which have their origin from Luther…not a one has a better appearance and greater external holiness than the Anabaptists. Other sects are for the most part riotous, bloodthirsty and given over to carnal lusts; not so the Anabaptists." Although, the Anabaptists agreed with much of Lutheranism such as *Sola Fide* and *Sola Scriptura*, they believed there were enough differences to warrant a different church.

According to Dr. Ellis Knox, history professor at Boise State University, even though Martin Luther started the Protestant Reformation, it was the French-speaking John Calvin (1509-1564) who made the greatest impact upon Western European and American evangelical and fundamentalist Christianity. Knox points out that if we did not have Martin Luther we would not have had John Calvin, but if we did not have John Calvin then the Protestant Reformation would only have been a German experience. Calvin was born in France and received a law degree in 1531. Just as Martin Luther experienced a spiritual conversion in 1519, John Calvin experienced a spiritual conversion thirteen years later in 1532. Calvin's theology was very similar to Martin Luther's, incorporating the principles of *Sola Fide* and *Sola Scriptura*, but they disagreed in other areas, such as the role of free will. Calvin promoted the doctrine of predestination, stating that human beings have no say in their salvation since we are predestined for heaven or hell.

Calvin's influence effectively spread throughout Western Europe and America because of two vehicles, his writings and his institutions of learning. Calvin's famous work, *Institutes of the Christian Religion*, became a reference book for Calvinist doctrine and for how reformed churches should operate. Because the printing industry was finally in full swing, Calvin's work reached all of Europe. Calvin also started religious academies promoting his theology. Students from these academies became highly educated in an illiterate world and traveled all across Europe evangelizing and starting up schools of religious learning for themselves. This guaranteed an effective evangelization of Calvinism, which directly influenced the later English Puritans, the Scottish Presbyterians, and the Dutch Reformed Church who eventually made their way to America.

Protestantism created a new problem for people attempting to honestly follow Christ's true teachings. In the Catholic Church, Christ is believed to have given this responsibility strictly to the body of bishops as a whole (Ecumenical Council) and to the Pope as head of the bishops, and members merely need to follow. The Protestant principle of *Sola Scriptura* means that one follows Christ's teachings by correctly interpreting Scripture, thus, the responsibility rests upon each individual. Infallible interpretation comes when someone receives inspiration from the Holy Spirit as they read Scripture. In effect, each person is now his or her own Pope.

As people became literate and finally had access to a Bible, they soon realized what educated theologians had already known. Interpreting Scripture is a very complex process. Calvin recognized this problem, and believed that a restrictive literal interpretation of Scripture was the solution. If we accept Scripture to be the sole religious authority, then the simplest, most literal interpretation is the only way everyone will agree. Calvin stated,

"Let us know that the true meaning of Scripture is the genuine and simple one, and let us embrace and hold it tightly. Let us...boldly set aside as deadly corruptions, those fictitious expositions which lead us away from the literal sense".

As evidenced by the splintering of Protestant Calvinist groups, the literal approach did not get all to agree. As a new splinter group defines its identity, it is only natural to become dogmatic about biblical interpretations favoring ones denominational theology.

As generations passed on from one to the next, leading members realized dogmatically accepted doctrinal beliefs might change in the future, which was an unacceptable prospect. This prompted the use of statements, or confessions, of faiths. Statements of faith are theological statements that define the beliefs of a particular denomination. Statements of faith by Calvinist groups caused the dogmatic practice of restrictive literalism to continue into modern times. For example, the English Puritan Westminster Confession of Faith of 1646 was a Calvinist instruction for the faithful to follow, which is directly connected to modern Confessions of Faith. American Presbyterian Synods adopted the Westminster Confession of faith as their doctrinal standard.

At times, this restrictive literal approach to interpretation caused tensions between the fledgling Protestant Christian reform movement and early science. Luther and Calvin lived at the same time as another important historical figure that made an impact upon modern astronomy, Nicholas Copernicus. In the 16th century, it was generally accepted that the Earth was the center of the universe, called a geocentric model of the universe. Christians embraced this, since a simple, strictly literal interpretation of the Book of Genesis seemed to support an Earth-centered universe. Besides, if man is the center of being, then it is only logical that his place of residence is the center of the universe. Copernicus promoted the idea that the Sun was the center of the solar system and the Earth revolved around the Sun, which became known as the Copernican model. This idea was first proposed by an ancient Greek named Aristarchus of Samos (310 BC-230 BC) over 2,000 years ago. If correct, then this would mean that the Earth is not the center of the universe. Luther scoffed at the idea. He stated:

> "This fool [Copernicus] wishes to reverse the entire science of astronomy; but sacred scripture tells us that Joshua commanded the sun to stand still, and not the earth." (1539)

According to science historian and professor of philosophy, Dr. Steven F. Mason, author of *A History of the Sciences*, John Calvin was also opposed to the new Copernican astronomy on the ground that it conflicted with a literal word of Scripture. Because of Calvin's and Luther's reaction, Copernicus entrusted his work to Andreas Osiander, a Lutheran clergyman in an attempt to avoid wholesale condemnation. On the year of Copernicus' death in 1543 his work, *On the Revolution of the Celestial Orbs*, was finally published. Osiander wrote the preface to the book, which attempted to make his theory more acceptable for those within the Lutheran Christian community.

Today, we can see that Luther and Calvin made a number of mistakes. First, they incorrectly believed that the Earth was the center of the solar system, and second, they misinterpreted Scripture in order to convince others of this belief. Instead of properly interpreting Scripture, they unknowingly manipulated Scripture in order to fit their religious opinion. Their followers most likely believed that all biblical interpretations from them were always infallible thanks to the inspiration of the Holy Spirit. In this case, they were led astray.

It is easy to see why Martin Luther misinterpreted Joshua 10:12-13. If you did not know that the Earth orbited the Sun, then the most logical literal interpretation is that the Earth is the center of the universe.

-"Then spake Joshua to the LORD in the day when the LORD delivered up the Amorites before the children of Israel, and he said in the sight of Israel, Sun, stand thou still upon Gibeon; and thou, Moon, in the valley of Ajalon. -And the sun stood still, and the moon stayed, until the people had avenged themselves upon their enemies. Is not this written in the book of Jasher? So the sun stood still in the midst of heaven, and hasted not to go down about a whole day." (KJV)

God is literally telling the reader that the Sun and the Moon stood still, "And the sun stood still, and the moon stayed..." Assuming that this event actually occurred, we now know that the actual phenomenon was the Earth ceasing to rotate, but this is not what God said. The only reason why we know the Earth must have ceased rotating is because of sources outside the Bible. Nicholas Copernicus was part of a revival in a revolutionary way of understanding the world, called empirical science. Observing and testing nature can now reveal its mysteries. Enacting the gods was no longer necessary. The act of searching for truth about nature by studying nature and not by interpreting Scripture was taking hold among certain groups within European society.

Most early scientists, or naturalists, in Europe lived at a time when it was automatically assumed that Noah's flood was a global event and that the Earth was only thousands of years old. There was no reason to question this, since the Book of Genesis is written with global terminology and that there was no external biblical source refuting it. In Calvinist reformed tradition, taking a restrictive literal approach to interpreting Scripture could be extended to natural events that occurred in the Bible. Biblical scholars in the Middle Ages now tackled the question of when the creation of the world occurred, and their sole source of evidence was the Bible, specifically, the Book of Genesis. Anglican Bishop of Armagh, James Ussher (1581-1656), determined the date of creation to be 4004 B.C., and explained his results in precise detail in his work, *Annalis Veteris et Novi Testamenti*

(1650). According to Simon Winchester, author of, *The Map That Changed the World* (2001), this was so convincing to Christian leaders since it was a product of a simple literal interpretation that Bibles in the 18th century placed "4004 B.C." in the left-hand column next to Genesis 1:1. Since 4004 B.C. was written in their Bible, this date for the beginning of the world now became gospel for literate Christians. In the minds of many, if it is written between the covers of their Bible, then it came from God.

According to Winchester, what sparked some naturalists to begin questioning these assumptions was an external biblical source, fossils. Fossils were found everywhere. They were made of rock, they seemed to imitate life, and they were imbedded into most rock layers, yet the Bible was completely silent about them. What are they? Where did they come from? How do they fit into Ussher's timeline of creation? In 1669, Nicolaus Steno (1638-1686) published his ideas about rock layers and fossils, and logically deduced that fossils are relics of life from the past imbedded into the layers of sediment as they died. Only later did these layers slowly turned into rock along with the dead organisms contained within them. For this to occur, the Earth must be much older than 6,000 years. This explanation was quite upsetting for Christian leaders embracing a restrictive literal approach to interpretation, because the Book of Genesis states that land was formed *before* life. The formation of the rocks could not have occurred after these creatures lived (and died). In the minds of theologians interpreting the Book of Genesis restrictively, Steno claiming that life existed before the formation of these rocks was an act of sacrilege. Nicolaus Steno was forced by the Copenhagen Lutheran bishops to accept Ussher's version of historical events. The social pressures were so great that Steno gave up the study of nature altogether, and took up a new career as a poacher and gamekeeper.

## America, the Beginning of Evangelicalism, and a Vision from God

In 1534, Henry VIII (1491-1547) took major stage in the religious reformation of England by separating from the Catholic Church with the signing of the "Act of Supremacy". Henry declared himself as the head of the new Church of England, or Anglican Church (now called the Protestant Episcopal Church). He broke from the Catholic Church when the Pope refused to annul his marriage to Catherine of Aragon. According to Dr. Christine Leigh Heyrman, professor of history at the University of Delaware, Henry had no intentions of following the reformed traditions of Martin Luther, John Calvin, or any other European reformed leader, but merely wanted to replace the Pope with himself as the head. Soon, reformed groups influenced by Calvin reached the shores of England and emerged from within the Anglican Church. They believed the Anglican Church did not reform enough and they wanted to cleanse, or purify, the Church. One such minority group was the Puritans. The Anglican leadership disapproved of their theology, which eventually led to their persecution. Two groups of Puritans and Calvinist reformers left England and made their way to North America. In 1620, the Pilgrims settled in Plymouth. They were also called "Separatists", because they cut their ties with the Anglican Church. Another group of reformers, the Puritans or Congregationalists, settled in Massachusetts Bay, Connecticut, and Rhode Island beginning in 1630. Later, a third group came from Scotland, and called themselves Presbyterians.

Dr. Mason points out in his book, *A History of the Sciences*, that reformers of the Protestant movement in the first few hundred years actually approved of this new scientific method, with a few exceptions as in the case of Martin Luther and Nicolaus Steno. Alternative ideas apart from the traditional Catholic views were seen as healthy. This relationship became less cordial beginning in the 18th century, because of an intellectual movement occurring in Europe and British North America, called the *Age of Enlightenment*. It promoted reason as the primary basis of authority, rather than the Bible. Many historians consider the Age of Enlightenment an extension of the Age of Reason, which began in Europe in the Early Middle Ages. Enlightenment thinkers believed that systematic and rational thinking could be applied to all areas of human activity, such as science, politics, the economy, and even religion. Trusting the head took precedence over trusting the heart. Some Protestant denominations, such as the Anglicans, did not feel a threat to their beliefs from Enlightenment philosophy, and actually incorporated it into their theology. Other Protestant denominations, especially the Calvinists, felt an immediate threat, especially because a number of Enlightened thinkers were denouncing the Calvinist idea of the "inherent depravity" of human nature.

As Enlightenment philosophy began to spread throughout Europe and the American colonial communities in the 18th century, this caused a religious counter-movement within the Calvinist denominations, such as the Congregationalists (Puritans), Presbyterians, Baptists, and Dutch Reformed. This counter-movement generated a religious revival, which lasted from approximately 1720 to approximately 1750. The revival in British North America is commonly called the *First Great Awakening*. According to Dr. Heyrman, it was a "revitalization of religious piety", and was centered upon the Calvinist doctrine of predestination. The revival's beginnings in British North America can be traced to the Presbyterians in Pennsylvania and New Jersey. Reverend William Tennent (1673-1746), a Scots-Irish immigrant, and his four sons, initiated religious revivals and trained clergy in the emotionally-based evangelical method. Spearheading the New England revival were noted Calvinist preachers, such as Jonathan Edwards and George Whitefield. Jonathan Edwards (1703-1758) was a colonial American Congregational minister, and was noted for his emotional fire-and-brimstone sermons. He is acknowledged by many to be the most influential evangelical theologian of the time. He and his followers were called the New Light Calvinists, rather than to the traditional Old Light Calvinists. Many traditional ministers disagreed with emphasizing the heart and a personal relationship with God. For example, Charles Chauncy, minister of the First Church (Congregational) of Boston, felt that the new enthusiasm was a form of spiritual derangement where emotions destroyed man's rational control of destiny.

George Whitefield (1714-1770) was born and educated in England, and was a cleric in the Church of England. Whitefield was originally involved with John Wesley and the Wesleyan revival within the Church of England, which resulted in the Methodist movement. He first went to America is 1738 and soon began his outdoor revival meetings. Whitefield was known for his powerful voice and his ability to appeal to the emotions of those in the crowd. It was estimated that tens of thousands would come to his outdoor revivals. This new style of emotionally-charged sermons, along with the outdoor revival meetings, was a significant factor in the First Great Awakening. Today's exciting evangelical preaching style can trace its origins to this religious revival. Anglicans, Quakers, and traditional Congregationalists and Presbyterians took exception to this new style of preaching. This caused a splintering effect within these Protestant groups, especially in New England. By 1750, the emotional style of preaching began to wane, yet the evangelical emphasis brought about by the First Great Awakening became a common thread between most Protestant denominations.

The 19th century in America also experienced a "revitalization of religious piety", which many historians have referred to as the *Second Great Awakening*. It lasted from the 1790's to around the 1840's. The United States of America had just become a new nation, and was undergoing major social changes. This period of uneasy change created conditions for another re-awakening. The highly energized evangelical method of preaching found its way back into Protestant preaching. Leading this new evangelical revival was Presbyterian minister Charles Grandison Finney (1792-1875). According to Dr. Donald Scott, history professor at Queens College in New York, a significant difference between this religious revival and the First Great Awakening was its shift away from Calvinist theology, specifically Predestination. Although evangelicals, such as Finney, did not completely abandon the doctrine of Predestination, they stressed that sin was a human action and everyone had the ability to receive God's grace and be saved, not just a select few. This means that free will had an important part in salvation. Additionally, there was an even greater emphasis placed upon public spiritual conversion at outdoor revival encampments. Historians estimate that Finney converted over half a million people. Less established Christian denominations, such as the Baptists and the Methodists, drew most of Finney's converts while the more established Presbyterians were not as successful. Much of the general geographic distribution of today's Protestant denominations and the style of evangelism can be attributed to the Second Great Awakening.

Independent Protestant religious movements also began as a result of this revival, such as Millerism (1830) and Mormonism (1830). Offshoots of Millerism are the Seventh-day Adventist Church (1863) and the Jehovah's Witnesses (1870). End-of-times prophecy now became an important religious issue in the early 19th century, especially for William Miller (1782-1849) founder of Millerism. Miller was a farmer in upstate New York after the War of 1812. He was originally a Deist (Enlightenment theology stating that God created the universe, but has been hands-off ever since), but after two years of private biblical study he had a conversion experience and became a Baptist minister. His passions were the prophecies in the Books of Daniel, Ezekiel, and Revelation. He believed that they contained coded information about the end of the world and the second coming of Jesus. By using his calculations, he predicted this event to occur between March 21, 1843, and March 21, 1844. Since he and his followers publically proclaimed Christ's advent, they were known as Adventists. Miller's calculations and predictions required a restrictive literal interpretation of the Bible, specifically, Ussher's chronology of creation beginning in 4004 BC. Within this chronology, Ussher recorded 457 BC as the return of Ezra to Jerusalem under the decree of Artaxerxes' seventh year, to restore the commonwealth of Judah under Jewish law. Add 2,300 years (Daniel 8:14) and you get the year 1843 AD. Interpretation needed to be restrictive, because allowing for any variation in Ussher's chronology would undermine the possibility of determining a specific date for the end-of-times.

Miller began evangelizing his end-of-times beliefs in 1831 and by 1833 he published his book, *Evidences from Scripture and History of the Second Coming of Christ about the Year 1843.* By 1843, Miller's predictions were well known to most people in America especially on the east coast, and his followers increased in numbers to over 100,000. They came from many different denominations, such as the Baptists, Presbyterians, Methodists, and Campbellites (an independent group evangelizing a return to the early apostolic church). When Jesus failed to appear between these two dates, Miller reluctantly endorsed the position of a group of his followers known as the "seventh-month movement", who claimed Christ would return on October 22, 1844 (in the seventh month of the Jewish calendar). This would be the last day of this age and the beginning of the "seventh day of the creation" age. Many followers abandoned their homes and jobs awaiting this event, which they called *The Blessed Hope.* When this event did not happen, Miller became disillusioned and gradually withdrew from leadership. He died soon after in 1849. The event was renamed *The Great Disappointment.* Dejected Adventists who found themselves leaderless then broke up into smaller splinter groups.

One such splinter group linked to Millerism is the Seventh-day Adventist Church. Adventist Ellen G. Harmon (1827-1925) with her soon-to-be husband, James White, teamed up with Joseph Bates, and founded the Seventh-day Adventist Church. Ellen White quickly became the spiritual leader of the church, and today is revered as a prophet. She believed October 22, 1844, did have a special meaning, but it was not the end-of-times as Miller had predicted. Ellen (Harmon)

White called this event *The Investigative Judgment*, which was when Jesus judged the living and the dead in Heaven. The second coming of Jesus on Earth will soon follow. Miller actually denounced this interpretation prior to his death. Ellen White claimed to have upwards of 2,000 visions from God with her first occurring just after The Great Disappointment in 1844. One particular vision was the beginning of creation. She states,

> "I was then carried back to the creation and was shown that the first week, in which God performed the work of creation in six days and rested on the seventh day, *was just like every other week*."

She then states that fossils were the result of the flood,

> "[humans, animals, and trees] were buried, and thus preserved as an evidence to later generations that the antediluvians perished by a flood. God designed that the discovery of these things should establish faith in inspired history; but... the things which God gave them [i.e., to us humans] as a benefit, they turn into a curse by making a wrong use of them [scientists]."

## Modernism, the Social Gospel Movement, and the Formation of Fundamentalism

By the mid to late 19th century, evangelicalism had successfully penetrated into the Protestant religious community, and became the established method of worship with emphasis placed upon spiritual conversion and free will. A lasting impact Millerism had upon the evangelical community as a whole was an increased emphasis placed upon end-of-times prophecy. Meanwhile, American society especially in the North was rapidly changing due to urbanization, increased immigration, industrialization, and capitalism. The intellectual community became further entrenched in reason, scientific thinking, and rationality. According to Dr. Nancy Ammerman, professor of Sociology of Religion at Boston University, science, technology, and business were eclipsing Protestant Christian tradition, prayer, and faith. As this was occurring, millions of European immigrants arrived with Catholic and Jewish traditions, creating an ever-increasing religious pluralism in America. Ammerman states, "Old assumptions (mostly Protestant) were being replaced by new dogmas of industrialism, historicism, and secularism. Religion gradually became compartmentalized in the private, family, and leisure spheres, leaving political and economic affairs to the secular experts." A new secular movement was beginning, which has its roots back in the Enlightenment Era. This intellectual trend formed the beginnings of what is called *Modernism*. It was a trend states Ammerman that "emphasized the power of human beings to create, improve, and reshape their environment with the aid of scientific knowledge, technology, and practical experimentation".

In 1859, the world was introduced to Charles Darwin (1809-1882) and his theory of evolution by natural selection with the publication of his book, *On the Origin of Species by Means of Natural Selection, or the Preservation of Favoured Races in the Struggle for Life* (also known in the abbreviated form as *Origin of Species*). Ideas about living organisms evolving from simpler extinct organisms actually predate Darwin by over two thousand years by an Ionian Greek named Anaximander of Miletus (610 BC – 546 BC), but it was he who discovered a convincing naturalistic explanation as to how organisms change over time. Soon after, it was evident that Darwin included the origin of human beings into his theory. Darwin's book caused less controversy than he feared, most likely because theories on biological evolution were already well known to the academic community as well as to the public. In 1844, Scottish journalist Robert Chambers had published in England his work called *Vestiges of the Natural History of Creation*, which dealt with the evolution of life and of the physical universe. It generated much controversy in conservative Victorian British society, but Chambers still gave the credit for creation to God, albeit a progressive creation. Within twenty years of Darwin's work being published almost every scientist was convinced of a naturalistic explanation to biological evolution, even though many still disagreed with his proposed natural selective process.

The publication of *Origin of Species* made such an impact upon American society that many, even in the religious community, accepted naturalistic evolution. In 1880, an American religious weekly publication stated that "perhaps a quarter, perhaps a half of the educated ministers in our leading Evangelical denominations" felt "that the story of the creation and fall of man, told in Genesis, is no more the recorded of actual occurrences than is the parable of the Prodigal Son."

Not all Christian leaders accepted Darwinian evolution, especially, conservative evangelicals. The threat Darwin created was not necessarily biological evolution, but the explanation behind it. Darwin suggested a purely naturalistic explanation requiring no divine intervention, or miracles. Conservative evangelicals believed Darwin was taking God out of the equation, which sounded to them like the modernist movement was now forcing its way into their Christian faith.

For many Protestant clergy, especially in the rural South, society was in a state of decay and sin was to blame. If personal sin could be battled with individual conversion, then societal sin could be battled with social conversion. Christian principles should work on society's problems. This belief created a new evangelical movement, called the *Social Gospel Movement*. Solomon Washington Gladden (1836-1918), minister of the First Congregational Church in Columbus, Ohio, was a pioneer in this movement. He called upon his parishioners to look beyond the promise of individual salvation, and focus upon transforming society. In 1883, a group of evangelical Christian Bible scholars met in Niagara-on-the-Lake, Ontario, at what was called the *Niagara Bible Conference*. This conference established specific fundamental Protestant Christian principles called the Niagara Creed, which was organized into 14-points. In doing so, it formalized the inter-denominational movement of Christian fundamentalism, even though this term was not yet used. There were concerns brought up at the conference about biological evolution and its implications for the accuracy of the Bible, but opinions were too varied for any consensus to be made.

Conservative evangelicals perceived another equally dangerous, if not more dangerous, threat to Christian society from modernism. This threat dealt not with the creation of life and the universe but with the creation of the Bible. In the 19th century, historians and linguists began to treat the Bible like any other ancient document, and applied the scientific method to researching its origins and formation. Instead of automatically assuming that Scripture was God's infallible work, they investigated its writings from a naturalistic perspective. This method of research was known as *higher criticism*. For evangelical Christians, this was just a slippery slope into believing the Bible was filled with man-made stories written without any divine inspiration.

Conservative evangelical clergy believed that it was now time to act before American society became too un-Christianized, so in the spirit of the Social Gospel Movement, a group of British and American Protestant theologians between 1910 and 1915 wrote a series of twelve volumes entitled *The Fundamentals: A Testimony to the Truth*. It is composed of the principles of conservative Protestant religious orthodoxy and evangelical practice, and it calls believers into action in both the political and the social arena. Out of it produced the "five fundamentals", in which conservative evangelicals used as their rallying cry. These five points of doctrine are: the inerrancy of the Bible, the virgin birth of Christ, the penal substitutionary interpretation of Christ's passion and death, the bodily resurrection of Christ, and the authenticity of the miracles recorded in the Bible. This not only affirmed traditional Christian doctrine for conservative evangelicals, but it also motivated ministers and theologians to take up the call.

Lyman Stewart, the head of the Union Oil Company, funded the effort for $250,000. About three million sets were distributed to English-speaking Protestant church workers around the world, which guaranteed that most Protestant religious leaders had access to *The Fundamentals*. In placing these beliefs into print, conservative evangelicals created fundamentalist dogma not open to reinterpretation or change. Generations earlier, the evangelical movement of the First Great Awakening was seen as the forward-looking progressive New Light approach to faith, while the traditional Old Light approach of the strict Calvinists was seen as backward-looking. Even though this "fundamentalist" movement was new, it was actually a backward-looking traditional approach yearning for the earlier days of Charles Grandison Finney and the Second Great Awakening before the decaying affects of modernism. Since biological evolution was believed to be a product of the modernist movement, it was seen as antichristian.

**Flood Geology and Social Darwinism**

Fundamentalist Christians at the time believed in creationist interpretations that were quite different than what today's fundamentalist Christians believe in. According to Dr. Numbers, most fundamentalist Christians believed in either Day-age creationism or the Gap Theory (ruin-and-restoration) creationism. Day-age creationists, such as William Bell Riley, interpret the Bible literally, but believe that the term, day (*yom* in Hebrew), used in Genesis means long geologic periods of time, rather than 24 hours. This belief is more closely aligned with today's theistic evolutionists' interpretation than young earth creationists' interpretation. Gap Theory creationists, such as Harry Rimmer and Cyrus Scofield (author of the popular Scofield Reference Bible), accept day as 24 hours but believe there was a long gap in time between the "in the beginning" part of Genesis 1:1 and "the Earth was without form and void." The Earth could indeed be millions or even billions of years old. What these early twentieth century creationists had in common was a rejection of naturalistic evolution.

One particular early twentieth century creationist, George McCready Price (1870-1963), was the key anti-evolution creationist most influential to today's young earth anti-evolution creationist movement even though his beliefs were considered on the fringe by fundamentalists at the time. Price promoted what he called *Flood Geology*. He claimed that geologists were completely wrong about the geologic history of the layered sedimentary rocks and the fossils they contained. While geologists were claiming that sedimentary rocks are the result of sediment (sand, clay, mud, etc.) being deposited and buried over millions of years, Price was claiming that they were flood sediments from Noah's global deluge approximately 4,000 years ago. The fossils were remnants of creatures that died during the global flood. He believed the Earth was created in 4004 BC just as Ussher had calculated using biblical chronology. This also meant that man was created fully formed, which precluded the possibility that biological evolution had any part in the origin of human beings. He began publishing his young earth flood geology literature in 1902 with, *Outlines of Modern Christianity and Modern Science*. In 1906 Price wrote, *Illogical Geology: The Weakest Point in the Evolution Theory*. He finished his most notable work in 1923, which was a college textbook entitled, *The New Geology*.

George McCready Price had no choice but to believe in a restrictive literal interpretation where God created the universe in 4004 BC for two reasons. First, Price was a member of the Seventh-day Adventist Church, and as stated earlier, central to their denominational doctrine is the year 1844, the Investigative Judgment, a date generated by the use of Ussher's biblical chronology. Second, the founder of Seventh-day Adventism, Ellen White, claimed to have received a vision from God, showing her the creation of the universe, which "was just like any other week." Accepting anything other than a young earth would be to deny Ellen White as a true prophet. If other literal interpretations were true, such as Day-age creationism and the Gap Theory, then this would mean the Seventh-day Adventist denomination is based upon error.

George McCready Price was not the first to come up with flood geology. The scientific community settled this issue at the beginning of the previous century. A convincing argument against a young earth literal interpretation of the Bible in the early 19th century was that no physical evidence for a global flood existed anywhere on the planet. A massive and violent global flood should visibly scar the surface of the Earth. English geologist and paleontologist (and originator of the Gap Theory) Reverend William Buckland (1784-1856) advanced flood geology and claimed in his published work in 1820, *Reliquiae diluvianae* (Relics of the Flood), that the gravel and till deposits spread across northern Europe and North America were the result of Noah's flood. As the first "official" geologist at Oxford University, Buckland was one of the most respected naturalists of his age. According to Dr. Steven J. Gould (1941-2002), paleontologist and biologist at Harvard University, Louis Agassiz (1807-1873) claimed Buckland was incorrect, and that the physical evidence clearly shows this debris came from continental glaciers. Within ten years and after numerous scientific debates, Buckland reluctantly agreed with Agassiz and rejected his own work.

At the time of Buckland's tenure at Oxford, another flood geology idea was discussed within the scientific community, which claimed that all of the world's layered sedimentary rocks were remnant global flood sediment. Buckland quickly discounted this hypothesis since it did not conform to the geologic evidence. In 1836, Buckland writes,

"Some have attempted to ascribe the formation of all the stratified rocks to the effects of the Mosaic Deluge; an opinion which is irreconcilable with the enormous thickness and almost infinite subdivisions of these strata, and with the numerous and regular successions which they contain of the remains of animals and vegetables, differing more an more widely from existing species, as the strata in which we find them are older, or place at greater depths."

According to Dr. Gould, the geology community as a whole rejected this type of flood geology, because it was "irreconcilable" with the physical evidence. As evidenced by Reverend Buckland, many well-respected experts within the scientific community in the early 19th century were devout Christians and had no difficulty referring to the Bible in scientific research. Even so, the 19th century scientific community was forced to conclude that there was no recent global flood, since there was no physical evidence to support it.

According to Dr. Numbers (a former Adventist himself), George McCready Price did not receive his education on flood geology from this early scientific debate. As stated earlier, Seventh-day Adventist founder, Ellen White, claimed to have seen in one of her 2,000 divine visions the rock layers and fossils being formed during Noah's flood. Price, believing White as a prophet, took this vision as gospel and developed young earth flood geology creationism around it.

Price and his vision-based flood geology did not convince most fundamentalists, yet they were all convinced of the societal dangers from naturalistic evolution. Fundamentalists began to organize and combat what they perceived as the decadence of a Christian society. If we were not made in the image of God, then Christian morality falls into doubt and that means there is no such thing as good and evil or right and wrong. If we are not responsible for our actions, then what will stop society from destroying itself? William Jennings Bryan (1860-1925), a proponent of Day-age creationism, was a powerful political figure at the beginning of the twentieth century. Bryan became the anti-evolution spokesperson for the fundamentalist community. He strongly believed naturalistic evolution was the root cause of the decadence of American society. He, along with other evangelical Christians, did not have to look too far to be convinced of the destructive power of evolutionary thought. The Roaring Twenties, or the Jazz Age, was a testament in their minds to the beginnings of our society's decay. Industrialism was changing our God-fearing way of life. Capitalists were justifying their relentless pursuit of power and money by claiming, survival of the fittest.

Bryan, as do many today, did not differentiate between two separate and distinct ideas, Darwinian evolution and Social Darwinism. Darwinian evolution deals only with the biological history of life. It is the hereditary change through time of a population of organisms brought about by natural selective pressures. It is blind to the future, and is merely reactionary to these environmental stresses. This means that it is not deterministic, which means that it has no future goals of the strongest or smartest surviving. Many times the weaker individuals survive to the next generation, because they have a certain characteristic that gives them a selective advantage at that particular time. For example, individuals plagued with the genetic disorder sickle-cell anemia have an increased resistance to malaria, a disease that kills between one and three million people annually. In this case, the sicker individual has a better chance of not dying, and is alive to pass on his genes to the next generation.

Social Darwinism is a social philosophy based upon *survival of the fittest*, a phrase never used by Charles Darwin. In this case, fittest means better. It is deterministic, because it has a future goal. The goal in Social Darwinism is to improve society. Of course, the person promoting the social change gets to define improve, and often this is done unfairly. It was used to justify social inequalities and racism. Hitler used this kind of philosophy to justify global expansionism. The Aryan race was obviously superior to all other races, thus they should rule the world and improve society. The father of Social Darwinism was an English philosopher named Herbert Spencer (1820-1903), and he inappropriately used biological evolution as a foundation for this social philosophy. His deterministic approach means that he improperly applied evolution to individual motives in human society. Incidentally, Spencer was the man who coined the phrase, *survival of the fittest*.

In the 1920's, William Jennings Bryan championed an aggressive anti-evolution counter movement, and put the issue onto the national forefront. Because of Bryan's influence, the Tennessee General Assembly passed an anti-evolution bill, called the Butler Act. It stated:

"... that it shall be unlawful for any teacher in any of the Universities, Normals and all other public schools of the State which are supported in whole or in part by the public school funds of the State, to teach any theory that denies the story of the Divine Creation of man as taught in the Bible, and to teach instead that man has descended from a lower order of animals."

This forced the famous Scopes-Monkey trial in Dayton, Tennessee, in 1925. The significance of this trial was that it opened the way for additional states to successfully pass anti-evolution bills. By the middle of the twentieth century, the majority of public schools were not teaching evolution in science classrooms.

**Sputnik and the Birth of Modern Creationism**

This was the way of things in America until a dramatic awakening occurred on October 5, 1957. The Soviet Union beat the United States into space by successfully launching the first satellite spacecraft, called Sputnik. This caused shockwaves throughout America. Our cold war enemy, the Soviet Union was perceived to be ahead of the

United States in science and technology, and public education was to blame. An immediate political and national movement changed what and how things were taught in public classrooms. In 1958, the National Defense Education Act was passed and quickly signed by President Eisenhower, and over a billion dollars was given to build a new science curriculum. States followed the lead of the federal government by adding their own financial support. Actual scientists now collaborated with science educators and set the guidelines for the science curriculum, and a new generation of science textbooks was being used. As a result, biological evolution was back into the public school science classroom.

For most in America in the late 1950's, the fear of an immediate Soviet domination took precedence over the fear that evolution was slowly destroying our social fabric, but not everyone believed this. Fundamentalist Christians had always maintained that the root cause of all social problems was this anti-God philosophy. In 1961, the anti-evolution fight was reenergized by the publication of one book, *The Genesis Flood* (1961). The authors, Henry Morris and John Whitcomb, Jr., were so convincing to fundamentalist Christians that it started a new creationist movement, in which they called *creation science*. Dr. Numbers comments upon this in his book, *Creationists: The Evolution of Scientific Creationism:*

"At last, in the late 1950's, a breakthrough occurred. John C. Whitcomb, Jr. (b. 1924), a theologian at Grace Theological Seminary (Winona Lake, Indiana) of the Grace Brethren denomination, and Henry M. Morris (b. 1918), a hydraulic engineer of Southern Baptist background, had each been moving in a creationist direction for quite a while before finding confirmation in Price's work. Each was also disturbed by a book published in 1954 by the evangelical Baptist theologian, Bernard Ramm, *The Christian View of Science and Scripture...* Soon after Whitcomb and Morris met each other they published The Genesis Flood (1961), an updating of Price's work, but one that, because of Whitcomb's theological contribution and Morris' scientific expertise, made Price's points more persuasively."

Morris and Whitcomb repackaged Prices' discarded flood geology creationism into something that the fundamentalist and evangelical community finally embraced. *The Genesis Flood* was an instant success with 29 reprints and sales in excess of 200,000 by the 1980's. It became the scientific support and justification for the belief in young earth creationism, especially since this movement was named creation science. One reason for its success, besides the more refined methods of persuasion in the book, is because Morris came from the mainline Baptist community rather than the fringe Seventh-day Adventist community as did Price. This made it more palatable for mainstream evangelicals. Morris and Whitcomb seemed to have predicted this Christian bias. In *The Genesis Flood* they do not credit George McCready Price's work, *The New* Geology (1923), as being their single most influential resource. Again, *The Genesis Flood* is merely an updated version of *The New Geology*. Don Stoner in his book *A New Look at an Old Earth*, states:

"The connection to Price and the Adventists worried Whitcomb and Morris…. Fearing that Price's Adventist-tinted reputation might hinder the acceptance of *The Genesis Flood*, Whitcomb and Morris tried to avoid any visible connection with Price. Although they left the substance of their arguments unchanged, they removed nearly every mention of Price's name from their book."

Timothy Martin points out in his book, *Beyond Creation Science*, that after 23 years and after the fundamentalist Christian community had fully embraced his book, Morris finally gives credit where credit is due. In his 1984 book, *History of Modern Creationism*, he states,

"I encountered his name in one of Harry Rimmer's books... and thereupon looked up his book *The New Geology* in the library at Rice Institute, where I was teaching at the time. This was in early 1943 and it was a life-changing experience for me."

The significance of their deception upon fellow believers cannot be overemphasized. In order to avoid the McCready Price connection, Morris and Whitcomb claimed that sedimentary rock flood geology was common knowledge even in early Christianity, and in so doing, hinted that this was the source of their modern sedimentary layer flood geology. On page 90 of *The Genesis Flood*, Morris and Whitcomb state,

"Before 1800, some of the outstanding theologians of the church were of the opinion that the Genesis Flood not only was universal in extent but also was responsible for the reshaping of the earth's surface, *including the formation of sedimentary strata*. Among those who held this view were Tertullian, Chrysostom, Augustine, and Luther."

This statement can be nothing but a deception. A thorough review of these early Christian's writings will demonstrate that they never commented upon sedimentary rock strata being the result of Noah's flood. Besides, Christian leaders prior to the 19th century believed Genesis clearly states that the land, which includes all sedimentary rocks, was formed BEFORE the creation of life. Since sedimentary rocks contain billions of fossils (evidence of life), it can only mean these rocks were formed AFTER life began.

# Chapter 4 – A Matter of Interpretation

*All meanings, we know, depend on the key of interpretation."*
-Mary Ann Evans (1819-1880)

## Misconception in Interpretation

Consider the following comment: "Scientists are mere humans, and have insignificant powers of reason as compared to God. Since the Bible is perfect, any man-made scientific theories that conflict with the Bible must be wrong." Many Christians strongly believe this claim, especially since the community of Christians that they associate with also believes this. Basically, it boils down to God's perfect revelation over man's limited ability to reason.

The above claim about revelation over reason has a major flaw in its logic. The comparison is not between God and man; the comparison is actually between man's interpretation of God's Word and man's interpretation of nature. When the words of the Bible enter your mind, you must interpret its content. Interpretation is unavoidable. Even the clearest Bible verses must be put into context, and this requires interpretation. Just as theologians interpret the facts of Scripture, scientists interpret the facts of nature. Ultimately, it is a case of human interpretation vs. human interpretation.

## God's Word is Clear

Years ago, I had the opportunity to listen to two friends arguing over a doctrinal issue within a Christian denomination they both belonged to. One of them quoted a verse in the Bible in support of their position and opened his argument by saying, "The Bible says… therefore, …" The other person countered this argument by saying,

"That's according to your interpretation. I believe the verse means…" Both friends quoted other biblical verses that supported their view. As I read the disputed verse and the supporting verses, it was quite evident that both interpretations could very well represent the true meaning. This made quite an impact upon me, because I realized that merely reading a biblical verse can fall short of discovering the true meaning behind the verse. This is a critical issue in the search for truth about the evolution/creation controversy, since it requires interpretation of both Scripture and nature. Human beings are fallible creatures. This kind of problem led former Yale president and scholar Jeremiah Day (1773-1867) to say:

> "The longer I live, the more faith I have in Providence [God's power and control over all things], and the less faith in my interpretation of Providence."

Regardless if the human authors of Scripture were guided by God or not, they have presented information in the Bible for future generations to read. This document contains the true intentions of the original authors, and it is up to later generations to figure out what they are. Theologians through the ages, such as Augustine, John Calvin, and Jeremiah Day have attempted to decipher the true meaning behind the verses. In other words, theologians use human reasoning skills as they attempt to reveal God's Word. Martin Luther detested human reasoning so much that he called it "Satan's whore". Luther pointed out the danger of theology, because it could ultimately lead to misdirection. An example of this was when Luther argued against the Anabaptist practice of "believer's baptism". Anabaptists performed a second baptism for those followers already baptized as infants, which led to the word Anabaptist (meaning re-baptizing). In modern terms, they believed baptism represented ones "born again" conversion of faith and the receiving of God's grace after reaching the "age of reason". According to Anabaptists, infant baptism was an irrelevant act. Luther believed this to be wrong, because waiting for the age of reason before being baptized meant human reason was a necessary step towards salvation. Luther believed that God's grace was a gift that had nothing to do with human reason, so infants can receive His grace during baptism.

Often times, Christians attempt to downplay the fact that human reasoning is required to interpret Scripture by claiming, "God's word is clear". It is a belief that the writings in the Bible are so self-evident that discovering the true meaning behind the verses requires minimal human reasoning skills. Because we are seeing the "plain truth", we have a direct connection to Scripture, *i.e.,* the true meaning behind his Word. It is an attempt to claim that theology is not required to understand Scripture. The problem with this line of reasoning is two-fold. First, as long as there is any level of human reasoning involved, there is no direct connection to the authors' true intentions. Theology is unavoidable. Second, the claim that the Bible is self-evident is simply wrong, especially as it relates to the history of life. The Bible, itself, explains the difficulty in understanding Scripture and the danger of misinterpretation:

-"So Philip ran to him, and heard him reading Isaiah the prophet, and asked, "Do you understand what you are reading?"
-And he said, "How can I, unless some one guides me?" And he invited Philip to come up and sit with him." (Acts 8:30-31)

-"And count the forbearance of our Lord as salvation. So also our beloved brother Paul wrote to you according to the wisdom given him, speaking of this as he does in all his letters. There are some things in them *hard to understand*, which the ignorant and unstable twist to their own destruction, as they do the other scriptures." (2 Peter 3:15-16)

-"With many such parables he spoke the word to them, as they were able to hear it; he did not speak to them without a parable, but privately to his own disciples he explained everything. (Mark 4:33-34)

Any fallible human being could have made a mistake in interpreting facts in the Bible just as easily as a scientist could have made a mistake in interpreting facts in nature. Martin Luther did it when he challenged Copernicus' revelation that the Sun was the center of the solar system. The existence of over 30 thousand Christian denominations is a testament to how common good Christians and theologians misinterpret Scripture. Followers in each denomination believe that the Holy Spirit has inspired their particular doctrine. This clearly demonstrates that misinterpretation of Scripture is more prevalent than most Christians want to admit. A feeling that the Holy Spirit is inspiring you may have nothing to do with actually being inspired by the Holy Spirit. When someone claims that the Holy Spirit has inspired their interpretation, they are also saying Christians just as faithful but with contradictory interpretations have not been inspired.

Many Christians believe that the Book of Genesis is a gift from God allowing us a glimpse into how he created the universe. If his purpose was to give us every detail and to be scientifically accurate, then Genesis would probably be too large to fit into a library. Instead, God explains all of creation in just a few short pages. Explaining the creation of life and the universe in a few pages requires a VERY general explanation. Being this general allows for many possible *literal* interpretations that still fit into the story. For example, there are literal interpretations claiming that the universe began 6,000 and even 10,000 years ago; while still others claim it began hundreds of thousands, millions, and even billions of years ago. A major misconception by those on both sides of the evolution/creation controversy is that "literal" strictly applies to the universe beginning only thousands of years ago, and this is just plain wrong.

## Inerrancy and Infallibility of the Bible

Recently, I was at a church service, and the pastor began his lesson by reading from the Gospel of Matthew chapter 19. When he finished he said, "This is where the King James translators got it wrong". Immediately, many at the service began to fidget in their seats after hearing something so unsettling to their core belief. I overheard one person angrily whisper to his wife, "This Bible is perfect!" The pastor then clarified himself by saying, "Now, before everyone lynches me, I want to clarify that I am not talking about God's Word. The original New Testament Bibles did not have chapters and verses. They were added later in order for us to better interpret his Word. The King James translators accidentally ended Matthew chapter 19 in the middle of the message that Jesus was giving. The message actually ends in the middle of Matthew chapter 20 (Matt 20:16)". After the pastor clarified what he meant, it was obvious that everyone in the church now understood and agreed with him. The last verse in Matthew chapter 19 states, "But many that are first will be last, and the last first" (Matt 19:30). In the middle of the next chapter, Matthew 20:16, it states, "So the last will be first, and the first last".

I was impressed with how the pastor skillfully approached a very sensitive issue in order to teach what he believed to be the real meaning of the message. The pastor was not attacking the infallibility of God's Word, but the fallibility of human translators. Before listening to the pastor's lesson, this part of Scripture always seemed confusing to me. Once the human corruption was revealed, the real meaning of the message became apparent. The pastor's interpretation of Matthew chapter 19 and 20 made sense. Even though the meaning of God's Word did not change, human corruption made it significantly more difficult to properly interpret His meaning.

For many Christians, the Bible is an inspiration to their Christian faith, and for some it is even more. It is actual Word of God, inerrant and infallible in every way, written down by men fully inspired by the

Holy Spirit. According to Webster's Dictionary, the word, *inerrant*, means *without error*, while the word, *infallible*, means *incapable of error.* These definitions seem clear-cut, which has inadvertently caused many Christian to have misconceptions about what their religious leaders have endorsed. When inerrant and infallible are applied to the Bible, they take on a spectrum of meanings. The definitions most often accepted and recited by fundamentalists and many evangelicals are those stated in *The Chicago Statement on Biblical Inerrancy.* In 1978, over 300 fundamentalist and evangelical theologians from a variety of Protestant denominations, such as the Reformed Church, Presbyterians, Lutherans, Baptists, and others, got together in Chicago and created an interdenominational statement of faith on biblical inerrancy. This inerrancy document has made such an impact upon fundamentalists that major fundamentalist organizations, such as the Evangelical Theological Society (ETS) and the Presbyterian Church of America (PCA), have formally adopted it. The Chicago Statement of Biblical Inerrancy explains inerrancy in its summary statement as,

"Being wholly and verbally God-given, Scripture is without error or fault in all its teaching, no less in what it states about God's acts in creation, about the events of world history, and about its own literary origins under God, than in its witness to God's saving grace in individual lives."

Article XII of the Articles of Affirmation and Denial section states, "We affirm that Scripture in its entirety is inerrant, being free from all falsehood, fraud, or deceit." It explains infallibility in Article IX as,

"We affirm that inspiration, though not conferring omniscience, guaranteed true and trustworthy utterance on all matters of which the Biblical authors were moved to speak and write."

Article XI expounds upon this stating, "We affirm that Scripture, having been given by divine inspiration, is infallible, so that, far from misleading us, it is true and reliable in all the matters it addresses."

The Chicago Statement of Biblical Inerrancy is an interdenominational statement of faith, but it came from the efforts of a single denomination, the Presbyterians. It finds its roots in the 1910-1915 fundamentalist statement of faith, called *The Fundamentals: A Testimony to the Truth*, which has as the first of its five fundamentals the inerrancy of the Bible. *The Fundamentals* were heavily influenced by the 1883 Niagara Bible Conference Creed from the Niagara Bible Conference organized by the General Assembly of the Presbyterian Church. It's first of fourteen point creeds state that Scripture is divinely inspired "provided such word is found in the original manuscripts." The Niagara Bible Conference Creed, being a product of Presbyterian ministry, is directly linked to the English Puritan Westminster Confession of Faith of 1646, in which the Scottish Presbyterians helped draft and finalize. Because of the English Civil War (1642-1649) the Puritans found themselves in control of the Anglican Church. One hundred twenty one Puritan clergy drafted the Westminster Confession of Faith as a Calvinist instruction/rule book for the Anglican Church to follow, which emphasized the sole authority and infallible inspiration of the Bible. During the 17th century, Presbyterians from Scotland, Ireland, and Wales, with loyalty to this confession of faith immigrated to America. By 1716, Presbyterians had finally organized themselves into large groups, or Synods. These Synods adopted the Westminster Confession as their doctrinal standard, which required all ministers to declare their approval.

Inerrancy has been a considerable sticking point for evangelicals in the last few centuries. According to Dr. John Battle, president of Western Reformed Seminary in Tacoma, Washington, the two most influential theologians on inerrancy as defined by the Chicago Statement of Biblical Inerrancy were Presbyterian theologians from Princeton Theological Seminary, Charles Hodge (1797-1878) and

Benjamin Breckinridge Warfield (1851-1921). Both eventually became president of Princeton Theological Seminary. Charles Hodge followed the lead of his role model, Archibald Alexander (1772-1851), the first president of the Princeton Theological Seminary. In the spirit of the Westminster Confession of Faith, Alexander defended the authenticity and inspiration of the Bible against 18th century Enlightenment thinkers. Questions about biblical inerrancy were raised during Hodge's tenure, which caused him to deal with the issue directly. In 1872, Hodge published a three-volume manuscript, called *Systematic Theology*. In it he states,

> "The Scriptures of the Old and New Testaments are the Word of God, written under the inspiration of the Holy Spirit, and are therefore infallible, and of divine authority in all things pertaining to faith and practice, and consequently free from all error whether of doctrine, fact, or precept."

Benjamin Breckinridge Warfield was appointed to the Charles Hodge Principle Chair at Princeton Theological Seminary in 1887, where he succeeded Hodge's son Archibald Alexander Hodge. He is considered the last of the Princeton theologians. Warfield was also firmly grounded in the Westminster Confession of Faith. He stated,

> "...defenders of the trustworthiness of the Scriptures have constantly asserted, together, that God gave the Bible as the errorless record of his will to men, and that he was, in his superabounding grace, preserved them to this hour-yea, and will preserve it for them to the end of time."

There is an important caveat in The Chicago Statement of Biblical Inerrancy's definition of inerrancy that many fundamentalists today do not realize. Many believe today's Bibles are perfectly inerrant, but The Chicago Statement of Biblical Inerrancy denies this level of interpretation. It affirms that only the lost original texts of Scripture were perfectly inerrant. Another name for an original text is an *autographical text*. Article X states,

> "We affirm that inspiration, strictly speaking, applies only to the autographic text of Scripture, which in the providence of God can be ascertained from available manuscripts with great accuracy. We further affirm that copies and translations of Scripture are the Word of God to the extent that they faithfully represent the original."

The greatest defenders of inerrancy in the 19th century, Charles Hodge and Benjamin Breckinridge Warfield, were both in complete agreement with this statement. Hodge stated that the Bible he was working with "may fairly be ascribed to errors of transcribers." Warfield believed inerrancy belonged "only to the genuine text of Scripture." Both also believed the last sentence of Article X that today's Bibles faithfully represent the original. Hodge states that not "one important fact or doctrine" has been affect. Warfield adds to this belief by stating that when we read today's Bibles, we are reading most of the autographic text.

> "We affirm that we have the autographic text; and not only we but all men may see it if they will; and that God has not permitted the Bible to become so hopelessly corrupt that it restoration to its original text is impossible. As a matter of fact, the great body of the Bible is, in it autographical text, in the worst copies of the original texts in circulation; practically the whole of it is in its autographic text in the best texts in circulation; and he who will may today read the autographic text in large stretches of Scripture without legitimate doubt."

Founders of modern creation science, Henry Morris and John Whitcomb, also agree that the only inspired Bible is the autographical texts. The very first sentence in chapter one of their book, *The Genesis Flood*, it states,

"In harmony with our conviction that the Bible is the infallible Word of God, verbally inspired in the original autographs..."

**Textual Corruptions and the Evolution/Creation Controversy**

Some of the most convincing arguments in the evolution/creation controversy are actually misconceptions caused by textual corruptions in today's English Bibles. Interestingly, these particular corruptions have no bearing upon the truth of biblical inerrancy as defined by the Chicago Statement of Biblical Inerrancy. Why is this? In the words Charles Hodge, textual corruptions of modern Bibles will never affect "divine authority in all things pertaining to faith and practice". Favored creationist interpretations are not included in this divine protection, thus, have the potential of being wrong. After all, there are multiple literal interpretations and they cannot all be correct. Case in point:

**1) The Solar Day**

Battle lines have been drawn by creationists about the interpretation of "day" in the Book of Genesis. Young earth creationists have claimed that the most basic understanding of "day" in Genesis is a 24-hour day, as stated in Genesis 1:5:

-"And God called the light Day, and the darkness he called Night. And the evening and the morning were *the* first day." (KJV)

This day is a solar day, or sunrise to sunrise, since it is modified by the words, light, darkness, evening, and morning. Creationists opposed to the young earth scenario, such as astronomer and evangelical Christian, Dr. Hugh Ross, suggests *yom* actually means millions of years. The English word, day, was not used in the original text, it was the equivalent Hebrew word, *yom*, since the text was written in ancient Hebrew. Dr. Ross points out that *yom* is not limited to just the sunrise to sunrise translation, though. It can mean the daylight portion of a 24-hour day, or sunrise to sunset. It can also mean an extended period of time as in "the day of the dinosaurs"; a 150 million year span of time.

In support of *yom* in the Book of Genesis meaning something other than a 24-hour period, Ross points out a critical problem. The Sun was not created until day four, yet there needs to be a Sun in order to have a sunrise to sunrise.

-"And God made two great lights; *the greater light to rule the day*, and the lesser light to rule the night: he made the stars also.
-And God set them in the firmament of the heaven to give light upon the earth,
 -And to rule over the day and over the night, and to divide the light from the darkness: and God saw that it was good.
-And the evening and the morning were the *fourth* day."
(Genesis 1:16-19 KJV)

To counter this argument, young earth creationists point to numerical adjectives used before the word, day, such as *fourth* day. They claim that whenever a numerical adjective is placed before the word day everywhere else in the Bible, it always refers to a 24-hour day. Genesis days referring to anything other than 24-hour days would be a contradiction in biblical literary style. Dr. Rodney Whitefield highlights this argument and comments upon biblical scholar, John MacArthur, referring to the numerical adjectives argument in his

Study Bible. MacArthur writes, "*Day* with numerical adjective in Hebrew always refers to a 24 hour period."

If this was the entire story, then it would be a very convincing counter-argument for those desiring a literal six-day interpretation. The problem is that it is not the entire story. First, a textual corruption has diminished this particular argument, and second, there IS another example in the Bible of day being used with a numerical adjective and not referring to 24 hours. Biblical scholar Gleason L. Archer, in *Encyclopedia of Bible Difficulties*, points out this textual error. Whitefield quotes Archer,

> "There were six major stages in this work of formation, and these stages are represented by successive days of a week. In this connection it is important to observe that none of the six creative days bears a definite article in the Hebrew text; the translations "*the* first day," "*the* second day," etc. are in error. The Hebrew says, "And the evening took place, and the morning took place, day one" (1:5). Hebrew expresses "the first day" by *hayyom harison*, but this text says simply *yom ehad* (one day).... The same is true with the rest of the six days; they all lack the definite article. Thus they are well adapted to a sequential pattern, rather than to strictly delimited units of time."

Whitefield points out that in the Hebrew text the Genesis days do not match in literary style with the 56 other times the Bible uses day with a numerical adjective. Every time numerical adjectives are used with day in the rest of the Bible they are modified with the definite article, *the*. English translators were mistaken and this led Christians to see a literal pattern that does not exist. The six creation days are unique, which suggests that they are not ordinary 24-hour days.

Even if we consider the King James Bible as inerrant, the young earth claim that numerical adjectives placed in front of days always refs to a 24-hour period is incorrect. Whitefield quotes biblical scholar, Norman L. Geisler, in *Baker Encyclopedia of Christian Apologetics*,

"Numbered days need not be solar. Neither is there a rule of Hebrew language demanding that all numbered days in a series refer to twenty four days. Even if there were no exceptions in the Old Testament, it would not mean that "day" in Genesis 1 could not refer to more than one twenty-four-hour-period. But there is another example in the Old Testament. Hosea 6:1-2.... Clearly the prophet is not speaking of solar "days" but of longer periods in the future. Yet he numbers the days in series."

Incidentally, the numerical adjective counter-argument still does not explain why a 24-hour sunrise to sunrise day can apply to the first three creation days when the Sun was not created until day four. In my opinion, the numerical adjective argument is a way to sidestep answering this tough question.

## 2) Fifteen Cubits

Most people do not realize it, but the Bible mentions how deep Noah's floodwaters were. Genesis 7:20 states:

-"Fifteen cubits upward did the waters prevail;" (KJV)

Since one cubit is roughly equivalent to eighteen inches, fifteen cubits is equivalent to approximately 22 feet. The simplest and most literal interpretation of this verse states that Noah's floodwaters rose up only to 22 feet. A flood of this magnitude could not completely inundate the entire planet, but it would do major damage to communities living at the mouth of the Tigris and Euphrates Rivers in Mesopotamia. Their "world" would have been devastated.

Young earth creationists claim that properly applied human logic points to a global flood, because of the mention of mountains and the use of global language. Note how Genesis 7:19-20 is written,

-"And the waters prevailed exceedingly upon the earth; and all the high hills*[Hebrew: heharim]*, that were under the whole heaven, were covered. Fifteen cubits upward did the waters prevail; and the mountains*[heharim]* were covered." (KJV)

-"And the waters prevailed exceedingly upon the earth; and all the high mountains*[heharim]* that were under the whole heaven were covered. Fifteen cubits upward did the waters prevail; and the mountains*[heharim]* were covered." (American Standard Version of 1901)

The founders of modern creation science and modern flood geology, Henry Morris and John Whitcomb, in their book *The Genesis Flood* state:

"The phrase "fifteen cubits upward did the waters prevail" does not mean that the Flood was only fifteen cubits (22 feet) deep, for the phrase is qualified by the one which immediately follows: "and the mountains were covered." Nor does it necessarily mean that the mountains were covered to a depth of only fifteen cubits, for this would require that all antediluvian mountains be exactly the same altitude.... Nearly all commentators agree that the phrase "fifteen cubits" in 7:20 must therefore refer to the draught of the Ark. In other words, the Ark sank into the water to a depth of fifteen cubits (just one-half of its total height) when fully laden."

The reason why Morris and Whitcomb did not accept the simplest literal interpretation of the clause "fifteen cubits upward did the waters prevail" is because of the word "mountains" in Genesis 7:19 & 20, however, the original Hebrew text does not say "mountains", it says *heharim*. *Heharim* can be translated as mountains, but it can also be translated as mounds, range of hills, or the hill country. For example, Psalm 121:1 translates *heharim* as hills: *Esa eynay el heharim mey'ayin yavo ezri* (I lift my eyes up to the hills). If we replace *heharim* with hills in Genesis 7:20 the second clause conforms to the simplest, most literal interpretation of the first clause:

-"Fifteen cubits upward did the waters prevail; and the hills were covered."

Interpreting *heharim* as hills would mean that the King James and the American Standard translators made a common mistake. Is there any evidence that supports this mistake in the translation of Genesis 7:19-20? Yes, compare Genesis 7:19 in the King James Version with it in the American Standard Version (used by Morris and Whitcomb).

-"And the waters prevailed exceedingly upon the earth; and all the high *hills[heharim]*, that were under the whole heaven, were covered." (KJV)

-"And the waters prevailed exceedingly upon the earth; and all the high *mountains[heharim]* that were under the whole heaven were covered." (American Standard Version).

Either the King James translators or the American Standard translators got it wrong. It may seem like a simple mistranslation, but it means the difference between a global flood and a local Mesopotamian flood.

A comparison of the words "prevailed" and "covered" used in Genesis 7:19 with them used in Genesis 7:20 demonstrates that Morris and Whitcomb's "draught" logic is flawed. Notice how Genesis 7:20 is merely a rephrasing of Genesis 7:19. This rephrasing is very obvious in the Hebrew Text and also in the American Standard Version, but since the King James Version has mixed the *heharim* translations it seems less obvious. "Exceedingly" is the equivalent modifier for "prevailed" in Genesis 7:19 as "15 cubits upward" is in Genesis 7:20. The "draught" logic was used with Genesis 7:20, but it holds no water when applied to Genesis 7:19. "15 cubits upward" clearly refers to the waters upon the earth and not the waters measured upon the Ark. This leaves only one possible conclusion. *Heharim* properly translates to hills, not mountains.

### 3) Be Fruitful and Multiply

Most people do not realize that when God commanded Noah and family to, "Be Fruitful and Multiply, and *replenish* the Earth" (Gen 9:1 *KJV*) this was actually the second time he used this commandment upon humans. The first time he used it was with Adam and Eve, "Be Fruitful, and multiply, and *replenish* the Earth" (Gen 1:28 *KJV*). The first thing that came to my mind was how strikingly similar these two verses are. They are identical. Maybe the circumstances are more similar than most people think, especially when theologians have claimed that whenever God repeats the identical phrase there is meaning behind it.

God commanded Noah to replenish, or repopulate, the Earth with his descendents, since he just destroyed all of mankind. Notice that God tells Adam to do the exact SAME thing. He does NOT tell Adam to "plenish" or to fill the Earth, which is what he would do if he were the very first man, but he tells Adam to repopulate the Earth with his descendents. This strongly suggests that *Homo sapiens* have been present on Earth prior to Adam, which conforms to the genetic evidence and evolutionary theory.

To counter this argument, creation scientists claim that the original Hebrew word for replenish, *male*, means both, to fill AND to refill. Additionally, when the King James Version was written in 1611, the English word, replenish, also meant, to fill. Their problem seems to be solved, but Genesis 1:22 conflicts with this argument.

-"And God blessed them, saying, be fruitful, and multiply, and *fill* the waters in the seas, and let fowl multiply in the earth".

Notice how the same phrase is used for sea creatures as it was with Adam and Noah with one exception. The English word "fill" is used rather than "replenish". The original Hebrew word, *male*, was used in Genesis 1:22, but the King James translators consciously used the word fill instead of replenish. If the translators intended replenish to mean fill, then they would have used fill just as they did in Genesis 1:22. The only way to get around this is that the King James translators made a textual error, but in this case, the context suggests otherwise. The reason I point this out is because it is an even stricter literal interpretation of Genesis than the young earth creationists' interpretation, yet it conforms perfectly to the genetic evidence.

It is also an example of how evaluating Scripture with dual revelation in mind discovers a better answer. Genetics has revealed that and ancestors of all modern humans left Africa in as little as two small group migration waves between 70,000 and 40,000 years ago, and these groups eventually populated the entire planet. Middle Eastern populations, which include the Israelites, carry African genetic markers (inherited mutations) in their DNA, yet African populations have no Middle Eastern genetic markers. This means Middle Eastern populations have an African origin and not vice versa. Geneticist Dr. Spencer Wells points out that according to the genetic evidence there is only one possible conclusion, the path was strictly one way out of Africa.

These examples make one point clear; discovering the truth about the history of the Earth by only interpreting Genesis is not a simple task, especially when taking textual corruptions into account. Also, a very broad historical document, such as Genesis, allows for multiple literal interpretations to conform to its description.

## Interpreting Global Language in the Bible

Young earth creationists embrace flood geology not because of the supporting physical evidence, but because it supports their favored interpretation of Genesis. In a sense, they are using dual revelation backwards by attempting to filter out scientific conclusions with biblical evidence. Again, we must assume that a particular biblical interpretation is correct, which negates this process as an effective truth-searching method. One piece of biblical evidence they use is global language. For example, they claim that the global language used in Genesis chapters seven and eight mandates an actual global flood. The language in the flood story suggests a global destruction,

-"And the waters prevailed exceedingly *upon the earth*; and all the high hills, that were *under the whole heaven*, were covered." (Gen 7:19 KJV).

For young earth creationists and other restrictive literalists "upon the earth" and "under the whole heaven", can be stated no plainer. God meant what he said. If we accept this line of thinking, though, we must accept it everywhere else in the Bible. Recall from chapter two what God said in Joshua 10:13:

-"*And the sun stood still, and the moon stayed*, until the people had avenged themselves upon their enemies. Is not this written in the book of Jasher? *So the sun stood still in the midst of heaven, and hasted not to go down about a whole day.*" (KJV)

How can this paradox be resolved yet still accept a literal translation of the Bible? The answer continues to be global language, but the early Israelites had a different idea of what global was. In other words, we must take into account the perspective of the people involved. It is equally convincing to believe that the human authors of the Old Testament thought the greater Middle East area was the entire world. Notice how distant countries, like China and Japan, are never mentioned in the Bible. Ancient Israelites did not know they existed. Language used in the Old Testament often refers to the "world" of the Old Testament characters and not to the entire world. In 1 Kings 4:35 it states that "all the kings of the Earth (eretz)" visited King Solomon to hear his wisdom. This can only refer to local kingdoms that had knowledge of Israel's existence. To them the whole earth was the entire "land" area known to the ancient Israelites (Egypt, Palestine, Ethiopia, Mesopotamia, *etc.*). Also, how could leaders from North America, New Guinea, and Australia visit Solomon? Is it logical to believe that the human authors knew that the earth was a massive spherical planet with a surface area of 197 million square miles? The Hebrew word for earth is *eretz* or *adamah,* and both of these words have multiple meanings, "earth, ground, land, dirt, soil, or country". In Genesis chapter one, God makes it clear that *eretz* means land:

-"God called the dry land Earth [*eretz*], and the <u>waters</u> that were gathered together he called <u>Seas</u>. And God saw that it was good." (Gen 1:10 KJV)

Just as he named the waters *seas*, he named the dry land earth [eretz]. The combination of the two is not called the earth. If God equates earth with land, then shouldn't we? To further demonstrate how "whole earth" is meant as a local land area, notice how it is used in the following biblical verses:

-"And the famine was over *all the face of the earth [eretz]:* and Joseph opened all the storehouses, and sold unto the Egyptians; and the famine waxed sore in the land of Egypt. -And all countries came into Egypt to Joseph for to buy corn; because that the famine was so sore *in all lands [eretz]."* (Gen 41:56,57 KJV)

In this case, *eretz* best represents lands (as demonstrated by the last three words of Gen 41:57). The global language phrase "under heaven" can also be seen in Scripture used in a local geographic area. Acts 2:5 states,

-"And there were dwelling at Jerusalem, Jews, devout men, out of every nation under heaven." (KJV)

Obviously, this use of global language refers only to nations having knowledge of Jerusalem. "Under heaven" used in Genesis 7:19 would conform to literary biblical style if referenced to a local Mesopotamian event.

The New Testament also uses this global literary style:

-"Again, the devil taketh him up into an exceeding high mountain, and sheweth him all the kingdoms of the world, and the glory of them" (Mat 4:8 KJV)

Believing that the phrase, "all the kingdoms of the world", actually does represent the entire earth, it suggests that God himself believes in a flat Earth. Regardless of how high the devil takes Jesus up a mountain, he cannot see the other side of a spherical Earth. If Jesus and the devil are both spiritual beings that can see everywhere, then the devil taking him up a mountain would be an irrelevant act. The purpose of taking Jesus up the mountain was to see farther, and the farthest one can see from a large mountain is a local area.

Many Christians, including evangelicals, believe a proper interpretation of Genesis conflicts with a global flood. Consider the following verses:

-" Also he [Noah] sent forth a dove from him, to see if the waters were abated from off the face of the ground;
- But the dove found no rest for the sole of her foot, and she returned unto him into the ark, *for the waters were on the face of the whole earth*: then he put forth his hand, and took her, and pulled her in unto him into the ark.
-And he stayed yet other *seven days*; and again he sent forth the dove out of the ark;
-And the dove came in to him in the evening; and, lo, *in her mouth was an olive leaf pluckt off:* so Noah knew that the waters were abated from off the earth." (Gen 8:8-11 KJV)

According to Genesis 8:8-11, the waters were on the face of the whole Earth less than seven days prior to the dove plucking an olive leaf off of an olive tree (or sapling). According to Dr. George Martin, professor of pomology at the University of California, olive seeds take up to three months to germinate. Under exceptional conditions, germination can occur in approximately one month. Moist soil, not saturated soil, is considered exceptional conditions. This points to a conflict with Noah's flood being global, since the dove retrieved the olive leaf within seven days of the waters finally abating off the Earth. Seven days *or less* is not enough time for an olive tree to germinate and then sprout to a large enough size to produce a leaf. Genesis 8:14 states that the earth was finally dried two months AFTER Noah left the ark. This paradox goes away if we consider Noah's flood as a local Mesopotamian event. If the dove made it to dry land that was not affected by the local massive flood, then this verse makes complete sense.

One argument presented against a local flood is that it does not make sense for God to tell Noah to build a huge ark in order to survive a local flood. He could have just told Noah to move away to higher ground. The problem with this argument is that it still does not explain the olive leaf paradox. Besides, this kind of logic seems to question God's omnipotence. If God is truly all-powerful, then he could have easily flooded the entire Earth and saved Noah's family and a selection of animals all on his own. The religious message behind the building of an ark and collecting animals more logically points to a lesson for mankind about obedience to God and an opportunity to repent. Medieval Jewish scholar, Rabbi Moshe ben Nachman (1194-1270), or Nachmanides, explained this from the perspective of Noah,

"I was told to build a large ark in order to attract attention and to cause people to enquire as to my reason for building a huge boat-and not even near a sea! I patiently explained my reason for building the Ark, and man had the opportunity to repent. Unfortunately, mankind did not heed the warning, and persevered in their wicked ways."

Also, God selected Noah, because "Noah found grace in the eyes of the LORD (Genesis 6:8 KJV). His Hebrew descendents were God's chosen people, who inherited this grace. The Old Testament is a history of these chosen people bound by the old covenant. God's intentions at this time focus upon them and their world, not the whole world.

# Chapter 5– As a Matter of Fact

*All we want are the facts, ma'am.* -Detective Joe Friday, *Dragnet* (1952-1970)

## Misconception in Facts

Is gravity a fact? Surprisingly, the answer is no, and just as surprising it never will be, regardless of the reality of its existence. If this is confusing, it is because we in everyday life often use the word, *fact*, differently than scientists do. We generally use it to mean an explanation that has been proven beyond all doubt. For us, if someone's explanation or argument is proven, then it is considered fact. For example, if the doctor diagnoses your ailment as the flu and explains it was caused by a flu virus, we consider this virus explanation a fact since it is accepted beyond any doubt. Scientists do not consider this explanation a fact; even though they are completely convinced it is correct. Fact in science has a different connotation than a proven explanation, equating it strictly to *observable evidence*. A scientific fact is not an explanation, it is the evidence used to support an explanation. In the case of gravity, a scientific fact is planets orbit the Sun or objects fall to the earth. The explanation of these facts is gravity.

We also use fact as to mean evidence, but not all evidence is created equal. Evidence used in arguments/claims fit into four general categories and each category has inherent strengths and weaknesses when it comes to searching for the truth. These categories are *hearsay-based*, *experience-based*, *authority-based*, and *empirical-based*. All can produce convincing results, but some do a better job than others in pointing to the truth. There is a scene in Tim Burton's 1999 film, *Sleepy Hollow*, which does an excellent job of showing the different categories of evidence, and how each gets used for the purpose of persuasion. New York City constable Ichabod Crane (Johnny Depp) is ordered to the small upstate New York town of Sleepy Hollow in the fall of 1799 to investigate three murders. The bodies were beheaded, and the locals are claiming that the killer is the dead headless horseman (Christopher Walken) coming out of the grave to terrorize the townspeople.

The scene takes place in Baltus Van Tassel's (Michael Gambon) study on the day Constable Crane arrives in Sleepy Hollow. Baltus Van Tassel gives Crane the history behind the headless horseman's death in the western woods twenty years earlier. He then states that the headless horseman has been haunting the western woods for the last twenty years, and has now come out of the grave killing the townspeople. Ichabod Crane expresses doubt that the headless horseman is the killer and says, "Are you saying, is that what you believe?" The notary, James Hardenbrook (Michael Gough), speaks in a scary tone and says, "Seeing is believing". The town reverend, Steenwick (Jeffrey Jones), then says, "They tell me that you brought books and trappings of scientific investigations. This [as he holds up the Holy Bible] is the only book I recommend you read!" Ichabod Crane takes a quick look inside the front cover then replies, "Murder needs no ghost to come from the grave. We have murder in New York without benefit of ghouls and goblins. The assassin is a man of flesh and blood, and I will discover him." In just one scene, Tim Burton expertly weaves the four categories of evidence into an entertaining scene. Van Tassel's history lesson about the headless horseman haunting the western woods are based upon *hearsay*, the notary's comments are based upon *experience*, the reverend's comments are based upon *authority*, and Crane's comments are based upon *empirical* data.

**Hearsay-based Evidence**

Hearsay-based evidence is a kind of evidence from the masses, and since so many people believe it then it must be true. Numbers give it credibility. Rumors fit into this category. Baltus Van Tassel's story about the haunting of the western woods was based upon the hearsay of others. Claims that are based upon hearsay evidence tend to start out with, "They say". For example, "They say that when a toad urinates on your hand you can get warts." The logic behind hearsay claims is not based upon testable physical data, but it is based upon the fact that so many people believe it. How could all of these people be wrong?

I remember years ago there was a Quaker Oats Life cereal commercial that had a stubborn young boy named Mikey fall in love with the cereal. As Mikey began enjoying his bowl of Life cereal, his brother says, "Hey Mikey! He likes it!" Soon after, everyone believed that the boy actor, John Gilchrist, who played Mikey died of eating a mixture of soda pop and Pop Rocks candy. Only much later into my adult life did I find out that John Gilchrist was alive and well and never even mixed soda pop and Pop Rocks candy. Once a false claim that is based upon hearsay evidence gets believed by a large number of people and goes viral, such as the Mikey claim, this misconception becomes an *urban legend*. The following are a number of faulty science urban legends that are generally accepted by the public:

1. *Toilets flush in the opposite direction in the southern hemisphere.* The Earth's rotation does have an apparent affect on the motion of fluids (Coriolis Effect), such as the direction of ocean currents and global wind patterns, but flushing toilets are too small to be affected. I personally tested this urban legend when I was underway onboard a Navy ship during my active duty days. While in the northern hemisphere in the Indian Ocean, I watched the water turn counterclockwise as the toilet flushed. When we finally transited into the southern hemisphere, I flushed the toilet and the water continued to turn counterclockwise. This demonstrated to me that toilet piping had a greater effect on flushing than the Earth's rotation.

2. *They say we only use 10% of our brain.* We use 100% of our brain. I have heard many very educated people start an argument with this urban legend as their primary piece of evidence. It is commonly used to support the possibility of an unknown part of the brain controlling extra sensory perception (ESP) or spiritual connections.

3. *A major earthquake will cause California to sink into the Pacific Ocean.* California does experience a large volume of earthquakes thanks to the San Andreas Fault system, but nothing is going to fall into the ocean. San Andreas Fault is a crustal transform boundary, where the North American crust is in contact and sliding past the Pacific Ocean crust. The western side of the fault system is slowly migrating towards Alaska, and not "falling" into the Pacific Ocean.

4. *Scientists are looking for a missing link.* The phrase, *missing link*, is a product of a misunderstanding of the evolutionary process. Missing link suggests that evolutionary change occurs like a chain where each chain link represents the next stage in evolution. The chain is a misleading metaphor for evolution, as is the ladder, where one species is supplanted by a more advanced species. This is a huge misconception, which has affected the evolution/creation controversy. Because of this, it will get further clarification in a later chapter.

5. *The Nile River flows up.* This urban legend is due to the confusion between north and up. Thanks to world maps being on the wall, the cardinal direction of north points up. The Nile River is one of a very few major rivers that flows north. It still flows down hill, because of gravity, but if we look at the river on a map it looks like it flows up.

Even though a particular piece of hearsay-based evidence may be correct, we cannot be guaranteed of its veracity. All too often it is just plain wrong. Because of this, science rejects any arguments that are supported by hearsay-based evidence.

## Experience-based Evidence

Experience is a powerful learning tool. Those that have created a Word document or a PowerPoint presentation on the computer learn quickly to press the save button periodically. Very few things are as depressing as working so hard on a computer project only to realize that it has completely disappeared because of the push of a wrong button or a power outage. Learning from experience has been an indispensable tool in the advancement of the human species. It was probably involved in man's discovery of the use of fire, the invention of wheel, taming the dog, and the development of agriculture. When an auto mechanic tells you that your alternator is not working, he is basing much of his claim upon his past experience in dealing with broken alternators. When he replaces the alternator and the problem is fixed, this increases his level of confidence in the power of experience-based evidence.

Experience-based evidence has its limits, because of what it really is. It is memory. When we use personal experiences as evidence to support an argument/claim, such as eyewitness accounts, it is now a thing of the past. Memory cannot be repeated in order to verify its authenticity and we must trust that the person's recollection is correct. The comment, "seeing is believing" used by the notary in the movie, *Sleepy Hollow*, was referring to eyewitness accounts, or other people's memory, of the headless horseman. The eyewitnesses may believe in the headless horseman because they supposedly observed him, but others must trust them. A colleague of mine, Jeff Gallo, demonstrates the weakness in "seeing-is-believing" experience-based evidence in his English classroom. He pulls out his keys from his pocket and throws them into a cabinet, then closes the door while the students are watching. He then asks, "Arc the keys in the cabinet?" The students reply, "yes", in which he then replies, "Prove it". How can they when what they experienced is now mere memory?

Our memory of an event and the actual event often times do not match up. Everyone has experienced faulty memory. We humans are fallible, and we may be just plain wrong. Every time we recall memories, there is a chance of what psychologists call *memory reconstruction*. When we remember a past experience, our mind is recalling the event from our long-term memory and transferring it to our conscious memory. In the process, it could get altered by our present thoughts, wishes, and it could even get mixed with other memories. Case in point: As a longtime disbeliever in the existence of ghosts, I have always felt that when someone sees or hears a ghost, it was merely a product of an incorrect interpretation of a perfectly natural event combined with a good imagination. The biggest reason why I was a disbeliever was because I had never personally experienced a ghostly event. Well, a few years ago at the age of 44, I finally had a ghostly experience. One evening just after midnight, I was brushing my teeth with the intention of going to bed. I was completely exhausted. As I was about to finish brushing, I heard my teenage daughter's basement bedroom door slam shut followed by someone running up the steps. I automatically assumed it was my daughter coming upstairs from her bedroom to use the bathroom before going to bed. Because of this, I quickly rinsed out my mouth out so that she could use the bathroom. My plan was to walk out of the bathroom and meet my daughter at the top of the stairs as she opened the stairs door, and then tell her the bathroom is available.

Just before I walked out of the bathroom, I heard the door at the top of the stairs close just five feet away from me. As I left the bathroom and entered the hallway next to the basement door, I looked up expecting to see my daughter, Brianna, in front of me, but that is not what happened. I clearly saw the image of a female turning the corner into the dark dining room no less than six feet in front of me. I only saw the backside and leg of this person, since the rest of the shape had already gone out of my view around the corner. It was definitely a female image, but it did not look like my daughter. It could have been a friend of my daughters sleeping over. Nevertheless, I still said, "Brianna", but there was no response. I had thought this person was headed upstairs to the second bathroom, so my plan was to stop the person and let them know the downstairs bathroom was now available. I spoke again, but there was still no response. As I walked into the dark dining room in pursuit, I heard her walking up the upstairs steps. I was then concerned, since a normal person would have responded to me. As I walked up the dark stairs, I noticed the upstairs hallway was completely dark. When I got upstairs, I purposely looked in each bedroom and in the bathroom while ensuring no one could go back downstairs without me knowing. I found no one except sleeping kids. The dog was in my sons' bedroom sleeping, so I knew no one entered that room. The only upstairs room that had a light on was the master bedroom where my wife was reading in bed. I opened the door and asked her if she just came upstairs. She nervously said no, since I apparently had a concerned look on my face. I then asked her if she heard anyone besides me walk upstairs, and she heard no one. I then walked back downstairs to my daughter's basement bedroom, and found her working on her computer. I asked if she had come up the stairs recently or had heard someone walk up the stairs, and she said no.

There are only two possibilities that can explain this sighting. The first is that I actually saw a ghost! What seems to support this possibility is that the experience was so real. What I saw matched in time and space with what I heard. The auditory experience, or sound, of someone coming up from downstairs caused me to respond by rinsing my mouth out faster, which I never would have done if I heard nothing. Also, my ego tells me that I can always tell the difference between reality and when my mind is playing tricks on me, so it cannot possibly be a figment of my imagination.

The second possibility is that it was a figment of my imagination. Admittedly, it was late and I was very tired, so my mind was not at peak performance. I just finished watching an action-packed science fiction movie, so my mind had been accepting fictional events as reality. My daughter heard no one come up the basement stairs, and my wife heard no one come up the upstairs stairs. Also, when I got up the stairs, my dog was sleeping in the bedroom doorway, and would have been awoken by a stranger walking up the stairs. It would seem that someone should have heard this if it was an actual event.

This experience is now just memory. I have recounted this story dozens of times, and every time I repeat the story it seems to get more and more exciting. This is reminiscent of the fish story, where the fish that got away gets bigger each and every time the story is retold. Have I inadvertently altered my memory in the process of giving the story more impact and entertainment? This is a definite possibility, although something certainly did cause me to hurry out of the bathroom. Because of this, I am confident I heard someone walking up the basement steps and I am also confident I saw a female leg walking into the dining room in the kitchen light. I believe this part of my memory has not undergone serious memory reconstruction. I am not so confident I heard someone walking up the upstairs steps, though. Have I added this later to make the story more exciting? I cannot say for absolute sure anymore. There is no way of repeating the event in order to confirm my recollection.

Incidentally, I am no longer a disbeliever in ghosts, and I call myself an open-minded fence-sitting skeptic. I am now open to the possibility of the existence of ghosts due mostly because the experience was so real. If I started out as a believer, then this event would have sealed my belief in the existence of ghosts. In one respect, my prior disbelief was hypocrisy. I did not believe in ghosts because I doubted anything other than the natural world, but at the same time I called myself a Christian, which requires a belief in the supernatural.

Not only can memory change after time it can also be created from scratch. For over 30 years many professional therapists have been practicing a therapy called *Recovered Memory Therapy*, where they place their patients under hypnosis in order to retrieve repressed memories from their past. Law enforcement has used this in the hopes of getting a witness to recall additional details of a crime. Those claiming to have experienced a close encounter with extraterrestrials have also used this technique in an attempt to bypass what believers see as "extraterrestrially-imposed" suppressed memories.

This therapy seemed to show promise, but a disturbing side effect began to occur. Dr. John F. Kihlstrom, describes a condition called *False Memory Syndrome*, where therapists inadvertently place faults memories into their patients during hypnosis. These faults memories were so strong that the patients completely believe in their authenticity. Chaplain Paul G. Durbin, Ph.D., Director of Pastoral Care Pendelton Memorial Methodist Hospital, explained a time when an Assembly of God minister sent his daughter to a counselor, because she was having difficulty sleeping. The counselor was the wife of a fellow Assembly of God minister, so he felt comfortable sending his daughter to her. After 64 or more counseling sessions that included the use of recovered memory therapy, his daughter claimed to have recovered repressed sexual abuse memories of her father abusing her between the ages of seven and eleven. She even remembered her father raping her and forcing her mother to watch. She also said that she had received a painful clothes-hanger abortion after her father impregnated her. The counselor believed in the recovered memory therapy technique, thus believed that the daughter was revealing the truth. Needless to say, the family's life went into turmoil. Her father vehemently denied all allegations, yet was forced out the church.

At the insistence of the minister's lawyer, the daughter had a physical exam, and it showed that she was still a virgin. Additionally, the minister had a vasectomy when the daughter was four years old. Her memories were false, which means this is a classic case of false memory syndrome. Clear cases of false memory syndrome have occurred so often that there is even an organization called False Memory Syndrome Foundations that has been formed by parents of adult children who had been falsely accurse of sexual abuse.

## Authority-based Evidence

When your auto mechanic explains to you that your car has a bad alternator, he is basing much of his claim upon experience, however, you are accepting his claim to be true based not upon your own experience but upon the auto mechanic's experience. Later, when you tell your spouse that the car has a bad alternator, the evidence to support this claim is authority-based. You are accepting as true the testimony from someone you consider an expert. Authority-based evidence has also been an essential part of human development. It is extremely effective for passing on knowledge and experience to the next generation, as in the case of a master/apprentice relationship. In my previous profession as a Navy pilot, much of my training was based upon authoritative instruction. To safely train me as a pilot in the shortest amount of time, training manuals and instructor pilots told me what to do and what not to do. Once I began flying, it was a combination of authoritative and experiential training. If I were told to learn strictly through experience, or trial and error, then training would probably have been extremely short by ending up in a crash.

Even though authority-based evidence is a powerful tool for learning, it has an equally powerful weakness. We must trust the expert and assume that their facts are correct, and often times they are wrong. For example, reading non-fiction books generally requires one to trust the facts the author is giving, unless time is spent validating them. If the author has ulterior motives other than truth, then trust in authority-based evidence has been exploited. The non-fiction book, *Holy Blood, Holy Grail* (1982), written by Michael Baigent, Richard Leigh, and Henry Lincoln, was one of the primary sources for Dan Brown's fictional novel, *The DaVinci Code* (2003). The authors of the *Holy Blood, Holy Grail* claimed that Jesus Christ married Mary Magdalene and had one or more children. Their descendents eventually made their way to southern France and began the Frankish Merovingian Dynasty, which ruled from 447 to 751 AD. Central to this was the existence of a secret society known as the Priory of Sion. Baigent, Leigh, and Lincoln claimed that the Priory of Sion was an Order devoted to returning the Merovingian Dynasty back to power in Europe and Jerusalem, thus, were protecting all known descendants of the dynasty. The authors of the *Holy Blood, Holy Grail* received this information on the Priory of Sion from a French journalist, named Jean-Luc Chaumeil. Chaumeil claimed to have received documents and information from Pierre Plantard, a supposed Merovingian claimant to the throne of France descended directly from King Dagobert II. Many readers of *Holy Blood, Holy Grail* accepted these facts as true.

In 1993, it was discovered that trust in authority-based evidence was exploited. Pierre Plantard confessed in court under oath that the Priory of Sion was a complete hoax. Recently, I watched the show called, *Digging For the Truth*, and this particular episode was dealing with the facts behind these claims. Josh Bernstein, the host, went to France and had a French scientist test DNA from the bones of an ancient Merovingian ruler. If the Merovingian rulers were descendants of Jesus, then the DNA will have markers unique to the Middle East. The DNA results showed only European markers and no Middle Eastern markers. This confirms that the Merovingian ancestry is purely European, and it also demonstrates that the Merovingian rulers were descended neither from Mary Magdalene nor Jesus.

Christians must recognize that evidence supporting one's religious beliefs is authority-based, from the beliefs of a specific denominational doctrine to the acceptance in an inerrant and infallible Bible. When we preface an argument by saying, "The Bible says", we are using authority-based evidence to support a particular argument. This does not mean the evidence is wrong, but we must remember there is a level of trust we have accepted in the authoritative source.

The general acceptance of authority-based evidence in society is one of the reasons why so many people do not understand the scientific process. Because most of us receive our science education through an authority-based process, such as from a teacher or from the news, we assume that science operates this same way. Many believe that scientists merely accept what other scientists conclude, yet this is simply not the case. Science actually rejects authority-based evidence for the same reason it rejects hearsay-based and evidence-based evidence. Anytime evidence cannot be verified, there is no way of disproving it if it is wrong.

**Empirical-based Evidence**

According to Dr. Steven Schafersman, a biologist and geologist at the University of Houston, Texas, empirical evidence is evidence that is *susceptible to one's senses (see, hear, touch, taste, or smell), so that it can be repeated and verified through testing.* An example of empirical evidence is DNA extracted from blood discovered at a crime scene. This piece of evidence can be tested against the DNA of a list of suspects. It is testable, repeatable, and verifiable. If someone questions the validity of the evidence, then they are able to test it themselves.

In the late 1980's, a couple of fellow pilots in my helicopter squadron were flying during a military exercise in the Pacific Ocean. Upon completion of the exercise, the helicopter was low on fuel, so they refueled with the nearest ship in the battle group before setting off to their own ship. While flying over the ocean, they began experiencing a loss of power, which resulted in a progressive loss of altitude. The helicopter continued to descend getting closer and closer to the ocean surface. They tried everything, but they could not find the cause to the power loss problem. They soon realized that ditching the helicopter in the ocean was the only alternative, so they contacted their home ship and made a forced landing on the water.

The crew was rescued without injury, but the helicopter had sunk to the bottom of the ocean. An investigation immediately followed to determine the cause of the loss of power. The crew claimed that there was no pilot error. The results of the investigation supported the crew's claim, which was based upon one key piece of empirical evidence. This testable and verifiable piece of evidence was a fuel sample collected from the ship that they refueled at prior the loss of power. The ship's aviation fuel had an excessive amount of salt water in it, which explained definitively why the helicopter had a loss of power.

Empirical evidence is the only kind of evidence of the four categories that is accepted in scientific research. Why do scientists put so much value upon empirical evidence and put so little value upon hearsay-based, experience-based, and authority-based evidence? The answer is verifiability. Scientific claims based strictly upon empirical evidence can now be falsified if false. The process can filter down to the truth, since a correct claim should never be falsified. If a claim has any supportive evidence that cannot be verified, then it cannot be falsified if false.

Is there a weakness in empirical evidence? Generally, science has no time constraints, but issues in everyday life often times do. If there is a time-critical decision to be made, then basing a decision strictly upon the available empirical evidence might cause a problem. Engineers sometimes have to follow hunches that are not based entirely upon the facts in order to solve a problem and save money for a company.

**"How do they know it happened in the past? They weren't there to see it."**

The Reverend Pat Robertson recently on his show, *The 700 Club*, argued, "How do they know it happened in the past? They weren't there to see it!" He was referring to the Big Bang Theory, the accepted scientific theory in astronomy that claims the universe began nearly 14 billion years ago. Reverend Robertson has been a vocal proponent of a universe beginning just a few thousand years ago, based upon his interpretation of the Book of Genesis. In view of the four categories of evidence, notice how his argument reveals he considers experience-based evidence much more credible than even empirical evidence. Observing the beginning of the universe is an example of eyewitness testimony, which would fit into experience-based evidence. It would be a complete surprise to him that if a scientist actually did see the beginning stages of the Big Bang the scientific community would reject it as evidence, since it is not empirical.

To demonstrate how the, "They weren't there to see it" argument is impractical even in the court of law; merely apply it to a murder case. If the requirement to convict murderers was to always SEE the murder, then crime scene investigations are pointless. Scores of convicted murders should then be released, because no one saw the act of murder. The reality is empirical evidence, such as DNA and fingerprint evidence, rates a higher level of confidence than eyewitness testimony.

Incidentally, the premise to the question is actually wrong in the case of the origin of the universe. Astronomers do see events happening in the ancient past. When we observe the Sun, we are not observing the actual Sun, but merely an image of the Sun. This image is approximately eight minutes old. This is because light (the image) travels through space at a set velocity, albeit extremely fast. If light could travel around the Earth, it would make six complete trips in just one second. Since the Sun is approximately 93 million miles away from the Earth, light completes the trip in eight minutes. Because of this, astronomers consider the distance to the Sun eight light-minutes away. Taken further, the average distance to Jupiter is approximately 43 light-minutes away. The distance to the nearest star to our Sun is approximately 4.3 light-years away. The distance to Polaris, the North Star, is just under 500 light-years away. If a super-advanced civilization inhabited a planet orbiting Polaris and was observing our planet Earth today with a huge telescope, they would be watching Christopher Columbus traveling to the new world. The point is that the farther away a celestial object is the farther back in time astronomers are looking as they view the image in the telescope. In 1987, a supernova explosion was observed in the sky in the southern hemisphere. This allowed astronomers to empirically test and confirm fundamental theories, such as the formation of heavier elements in supernova explosions. This particular supernova was approximately 175,000 light-years away, which means that they were observing an event that took place 175,000 years ago.

# Chapter 6 - The Self-Correcting Process of Science

*Science is built up of facts, as a house is built of stones; but an accumulation of facts is no more a science than a heap of stones is a house.* -Henri Poincaré (Science and Hypothesis, 1905)

## A House Built Upon Reliable Knowledge

A close friend once told me, "Why believe what the scientists are saying? It's only going to change again in ten years." If people had a better understanding of the scientific process, then it would be apparent this statement is off the mark. It is not that scientific conclusions merely change with the wind; it is that science is a dynamic process of eliminating incorrect ideas as new evidence is taken into account. It never forgets the earlier incorrect ideas. As this filtering process continues, conclusions cannot help but be closer to the truth as new discoveries are made. Science is a self-correcting process towards the truth. Proof is in the pudding. Notice how advances in science and technology are occurring at such an accelerated rate in the last century.

Modern science is filled with examples of how this process has filtered out human error, and even deception. The Piltdown Man fraud is used by many religiously motivated activists as to show the weakness and fallibility of science, but the fraud actually demonstrates its biggest strength, the self-correcting process. Scientists, Kenneth Oakley, J. S. Weiner, and W. E. le Gros Clark, in 1953 discovered the fraud by using the same rigorous process that has discovered answers about human ancestry.

Between 1908 and 1912, lawyer and amateur anthropology enthusiast, Charles Dawson, along with his friend, Pierre Teilhard de Chardin, a French Jesuit priest and future paleontologist, discovered near Piltdown, England, a possible human ancestor. It possessed a very human-like skull with a large brain and a very ape-like jaw. After three years of digging and collecting, Dawson finally contacted a paleontology professional, Arthur Smith Woodward, keeper of paleontology at the British Museum. Woodward was already a proponent of the hypothesis that brain size evolved first in our human ancestors, and Piltdown Man supported this hypothesis. Woodward recognized the importance of the find, and became personally involved. The discovery was named *Eoanthropus dawsoni,* or Piltdown Man, and Woodward published the discovery in December 1912.

The find was initially met with skepticism, such as with the famous French physical anthropologist, Marcellin Boule and the leading American paleontologist, H. F. Osborn. Then, in January 1915, Dawson conveniently discovered further evidence in a second site two miles away from the first site. This paved the way for general acceptance within the European and American scientific communities.

In 1924, Raymond Dart, an Australian anatomy professor in Johannesburg, South Africa, came across a new human ancestor find that seemed to contradict Piltdown Man. He came into possession of a recently excavated fossilized skull of a 3-4 year old ape-like creature that had a chimp-sized brain, it possessed human-like teeth, and had a foramen magnum that indicated this creature walked like humans (bipedal) and not like all other apes (quadrupedal). It possessed human-like features and ape-like features, so Dart concluded that this was a fossil hominid. Dart named this discovery, *Australopithecus africanus* (man/ape of southern Africa), and affectionately called it, the Taung Child.

The reason why this find contradicted the Piltdown find was that it showed brain size was a later evolutionary development than other morphological features, such as bipedalism and canine reduction. Piltdown, on the other hand, suggested brain size was the first evolutionary development.

To Dart's dismay, the English scientific establishment scoffed at this new idea, because it contradicted their "brain size first" theory.

Additionally, England would no longer be part of the picture in the development of humans. This eventually created two camps, those who accepted Piltdown Man and those who accepted the Taung Child. As time went by, many began to suspect a Piltdown fraud for a number of reasons. First, there were no more English discoveries by anyone but Dawson. Second, in 1936, an adult *Australopithecus africanus* was discovered in South Africa, which supported Raymond Dart's discovery. In 1953, testing on Piltdown Man was finally approved. Oakley, Weiner, and Clark proved that the Piltdown bones had been chemically stained to make them look ancient, and they found that the teeth were filed down to make it look like human wear. Piltdown Man was actually a modern human skull fitted with an orangutan jaw. Also, the discovered flint tools had actually been recently carved. Even though bias and deception kept the Piltdown hoax going for around 40 years, the scientific process eventually filtered it out.

According to Dr. Schafersman, science demands a certain type of knowledge to build upon called *reliable knowledge*. Reliable knowledge is simply the knowledge gained by the scientific community through science's self-corrective process. This self-corrective nature allows for the next stage in discovery, the building of the house of knowledge. We can now ask even deeper questions that the previous generations did not even know to ask. Michel de Montaigne once stated, "We can be knowledgeable with other men's knowledge, but we cannot be wise with other men's wisdom." This quote was designed to show the value of wisdom, but is also hints at one of the secrets of success of science. Wisdom is limited to a particular individual's understanding, while knowledge is open to all and has no limits as it builds upon itself. We did not know that off the coast of Seattle, Washington, magnitude 9.0 earthquakes have happened in the past and will happen in the near future until the world experienced the Great Sumatra Earthquake of 2004. Recently, we discovered Seattle's underwater geology is almost identical to the geology off the coast of Sumatra. Asking questions about nature has improved the understanding of the geology of the coast of Washington, and it may possibly save lives in the future.

## Misconceptions about Science

In 2002, I wrote a rebuttal in the Buffalo News to an anti-evolution commentary on the evolution/creation controversy. The article I responded to was titled; *Theory of Evolution is just that, a theory*, which was in the February 22, 2002 Sunday edition. The author's point was that evolution is *just* a theory, and should not be elevated to the status of a great truth. The following is my response to this article, which was edited by a colleague of mine, Bruce Adams, and then published in the Buffalo News on March 15, 2002:

"In Richard's attempt to refute evolution, he wrote that evolution is just a theory, referring to it as "bad science." As a science teacher, I wonder if Richard knows what good science is. He apparently falls prey to two erroneous assertions that creationists are fond of making. The first is that a theory is "just a guess." The second is that theories, if "proven", become facts. Both claims demonstrate a failure to understand the scientific process. In science, when a question is posed such as, "Why are elephant and dinosaur fossils never found together?" Scientists apply knowledge and experience to arrive at an explanation. This explanation is called a hypothesis; an educated "guess" not yet confirmed. To confirm a hypothesis, evidence is gathered in the form of fact – pieces of data – that either support or refute it. If they do not support the hypothesis, it is discarded. If they do, a theory is born. Unlike a guess, a theory must be supported by evidence. But that's not the end of the process. The theory is then published in a professional journal for peer review so that the rest of the world can attempt to shoot holes through it. Here is where theories really survive or fail. The statement, "once a theory is proven, then it is a fact" is actually "bad science." Is gravity a fact? No, and it will never be. What is a fact, is that things fall. The accepted explanation, supported by facts, is called gravity. Does Richard consider gravity unproven? The beauty of science is that it is self-correcting. If the facts refute a theory, it is eliminated. Evolutionary theory has been scrutinized by experts for more than 150 years, and it continues to survive as the only fact-based explanation for the diversity of life."

In recent years anti-evolution creationists, specifically intelligent design (ID) proponents, have been attempting to legislate equal time for creationism and evolution in the public science classroom. Their central argument is the same "just a theory" ploy I rebutted in the Buffalo News in 2002. This argument exploits one of the biggest misconceptions about modern science. It states that the scientific process begins with a hypothesis, or educated guess. Once the hypothesis is taken seriously, it gets renamed to a theory, although it is still based mostly upon conjecture. Once the theory gets proven with evidence, it is then raised to the level of fact. Finally, if it gets proven beyond all doubt, then it is called a law, as in the Law of Thermodynamics. Although, this is a very common belief of how science works, it is completely wrong. The following are the same scientific terms as defined by the National Academy of Sciences:

*Scientific Fact*: an observation that has been repeatedly confirmed, and is accepted as true. It is also called empirical evidence or data. The key here is verifiability. If it cannot be observed and tested, then it is not a scientific fact. Facts are NOT explanations, as was discussed in the previous chapter.

*a. Hypothesis*: A tentative statement about the natural world leading to deductions that can be tested. This statement is an educated *explanation* that has the ability to be tested.

*b. Theory*: A well-substantiated (*tested*) explanation of some aspect of the natural world that can incorporate facts, laws, and hypotheses.

*c. Law*: A descriptive generalization about how some aspect of the natural world behaves under stated circumstances. It is a *description*, not an explanation.

Theories are tested fact-based explanations, and are the end result of scientific research. Theories do not turn into facts, nor do they turn into laws. Theories explain while laws describe. In the case of gravity, it is a theory because it explains why things fall to the ground. It is also a law, because we can describe the gravitational processes mathematically. For example, using the mathematical laws of gravity, we can calculate the mass of the Earth.

**General Assumption**

A major reason why the scientific community rejects creation science as a valid science is because its approach has an admitted bias. Creation science begins with a bias, the belief that their interpretation of Genesis is correct, and then it attempts to justify this opinion with selective evidence. To counter this assertion, creation scientists say that they are merely starting out with a general assumption just as scientists do and that the scientists' assumption is biased against God. They claim they start with the general assumption that God created the Earth (thus, God must be part of the scientific explanation) and scientists start with the general assumption that there is no God, thus no supernatural involvement. An example of this is televangelist James Dobson's claim that science standards use a little-known rule to censor the evidence for design by God called *methodological naturalism.* He states that if it is required that natural effects have natural causes, then God cannot be part of the equation.

This sounds quite logical, but it is actually misrepresents the issue. There IS a general assumption that must be used in science, but it is not that there is no God. What is the real general assumption in accordance with methodological naturalism?

*-Natural laws are sufficient to account for all observations in nature and that supernatural origins are beyond the scope of the scientific method.*

This assumption does not take God out of the equation. In a Christian perspective, this general assumption means that the natural laws God put into place for the existence of reality are able to act without any divine disturbance. The idea that God put into place natural laws that require no divine tweaking seems to demonstrate a greater faith in his omnipotence than the anti-evolution creationists' view of a special creation violating all of God's own natural laws.

To not have this general assumption would make the scientific process useless in discovering the truth about nature. It is a GENERAL assumption that merely tells the participants the arena to work within when they are answering SPECIFIC questions about nature. Sir Isaac Newton, a favored scientists creation scientists love to quote, stated it this way,

"We are to admit no more causes of natural things than such as are both true and sufficient to explain their appearances. Therefore to the same natural effects we must, as far as possible, assign the same causes."

## Where Logic Meets Truth

Thanks to causality, or the principle of cause and effect, the use of logic and logical arguments are an effective pathway to truth, and is a critical step in the scientific process. This leads to a question. Just because our logical thinking has caused us to be convinced of our position in an argument, does this guarantee that we are closer to the truth? Have you ever been completely convinced of something, only to find out that you were completely wrong? It happens to everyone, and this demonstrates that being convinced may or may not have anything to do with the truth. A logical argument can be defined as, "when the conclusion *unavoidably* follows from the statements of fact, or facts (premises)." It is not defined as, "when the conclusion *convincingly* follows from the facts."

A logical argument requires two elements; it must be *valid* and it must be *sound*. Philosophy professor, Dr. James Mahon, from Washington and Lee University explains it with the following two statements:

*1)  All arguments are either invalid or valid;*
*2)  All valid arguments are either unsound or sound.*

A valid argument means that if the facts are true, then the conclusion is true. Professor Mahon states, "If you accept the statements of fact, then you must accept the conclusion, or else you are contradicting yourself." This does not guarantee truth, though. An argument can be wrong, yet still be valid if any of the facts are false. A sound argument means that the argument is valid AND all of the statements of fact are right. According to professor Mahon, "If an argument is sound, then the conclusion must be true." If an argument is considered sound, then you are probably that much closer to the truth. Logic is a mandatory step in the scientific process, since the goal is to find the truth once the facts are collected. In order for the scientific community to consider a scientific claim as sound, the statements of fact must be verifiable and the arguments must be evaluated.

The above deductive logical approach is called the *rational approach* where there are inherent truths that can be reasoned out. Science uses this approach along with an inductive logical approach called the *empirical approach*. The empirical approach evaluates empirical evidence in order to glean out patterns and discover new truths. An analogy of this approach is when puzzle pieces are placed in a puzzle and a picture begins to reveal itself. I used this approach in my graduate fieldwork when I collected thousands of fossils, paying particular attention to which type of sedimentary rocks they were discovered in. This revealed a number of patterns unknown to science before I discovered them.

## Cherry Picking the Facts

John Quincy Adams once stated, "Facts are stubborn things; and whatever may be our wishes, our inclinations, or the dictates of our passions, they cannot alter the state of facts and evidence." Emphasizing empirical evidence effectively promotes objectivity in the scientific process for the reason John Quincy Adams commented upon, but there is still the problem of manipulation of this evidence. *Cherry picking* is the act of being selective with the facts in order to make an unsound argument seem sound. The goal of someone using this tactic is not necessarily to discover the truth, but to convince others of a personal agenda. Picked cherries in the basket have gone through a selective process, and do not necessarily represent the cherries available on the whole tree. The undesirable cherries are still on the tree or are discarded. This metaphor closely models someone with a hidden agenda trying to persuade an audience by using selected facts. The argument may be very convincing, but ALL of the facts were not taken into account. If they were, then it would be a case of convoluted logic.

Politics is a social arena where cherry picking is common. For example, just before a local school budget vote in my school district, I received in the mail a "Vote No" piece of propaganda. Although, the comments seemed very convincing due to their validity, some of the claims were faulty. For example, it claimed that the public voted for a zero percent raise last year, prompting the school district to secretly and deceptively raise taxes by a few percent. This is deceptive. Our community did not vote "yes" to a zero percent raise in the school budget, but they voted "no" to a 6% raise. What they failed to mention is that a state-mandated contingency budget automatically goes into effect, which accounts for the few percent raise. The school was doing nothing secretly, but merely abiding by state law. Notice that their agenda was not to inform the public of truth, but it was to convince the public to vote no.

## Confirmation Bias

Biases are any of a wide range of observer effects identified in cognitive science and social psychology that cause partiality of one thing over another. One type is visual bias. It occurs when viewing a Hubble Space Telescope photo of hundreds of galaxies in close proximity to each other. There are three general types of galaxies, irregular, elliptical, and spiral galaxies. By viewing the photo, it would seem that the spiral galaxy is the most common type, but it is not. The spiral shape catches the eye more than the other shapes, which creates a visual illusion.

Even if we have the most honest intentions in seeking the truth, human beings have an inherent tendency to emphasize facts that confirm their beliefs and a tendency to de-emphasize facts that do not. Psychologists call this type of bias, *confirmation bias*. For example, if you believe that you get sick more often during a full moon phase and the next time you get sick is coincidentally during a full moon, this confirms and reinforces your belief. You probably get sick equally at times other than a full moon, but those times tend to be ignored. Scientists are human, too, and even though they may have been trained to be objective, confirmation bias creeps in. They recognized this early on in the development of modern science, which is why a process of peer review has been incorporated. In order for scientific research to get published in a professional peer reviewed journal, the research is sent to selected experts in that particular scientific field to scrutinize it. Their job is to make sure all of the evidence is empirical, ensure the facts unavoidably follow to the conclusion, and to weed out any conjecture. Ultimately, they are looking for any evidence of confirmation bias. If they find some, it gets rejected until the research is corrected.

**The Power of Prediction**

One of the greatest benefits that the scientific process has in discovering the truth about nature is its ability to predict. Because natural forces govern the universe through causality, nature is predictable. Science can predict the natural effects of natural causes. For example, thanks to Kepler's Laws of Planetary Motion, we can predict where Jupiter will be in its orbit in 3,000 years. We can predict when our Sun will exhaust its hydrogen nuclear fuel in its core and become a red giant. If the prediction does not occur, then this is evidence an original scientific claim is invalid.

One of my favorite examples of the power of scientific prediction occurred in 1965, because of how clearly unbiased the outcome was. In 1964, Arno Penzias and Robert Wilson, working at Bell Labs in Holmdel, New Jersey, were experimenting with a new microwave telescope to detect radio waves bouncing off echo balloon satellites. The instrument kept on receiving steady electromagnetic static, or noise, at a wavelength of 1.9 millimeters. They initially thought it was some kind of interference, such as pigeon droppings in the huge horn-shaped receiver. After cleaning the droppings, they still had the

1.9-millimeter noise. The noise was occurring continuously day and night, and it was evenly spaced throughout the entire sky. They finally concluded that this noise came from outer space, and it most likely originated from outside our galaxy.

At the same time just forty miles away, three astrophysicists, Robert Dicke, Jim Peebles, and David Wilkinson, at Princeton University were attempting to search for remnant radiation from the beginning of the universe. Early 20th century physicists predicted mathematically that if the Big Bang theory is correct, we should find 2-millimeter microwave energy hitting the Earth in all directions. The Big Bang theory states that when the universe was infinitesimally small it existed at temperatures exceeding one trillion degrees. At this temperature, matter cannot exist and the only thing that can is the most intense electromagnetic energy, called gamma radiation. Albert Einstein explained with his famous formula, $E=MC^2$, that matter and energy are the same thing just existing in different states depending upon temperature. As the universe began its expansion, gamma radiation stretched out and cooled allowing much of the energy to convert into matter. Some of the radiation stayed as electromagnetic energy and continued to stretch out into less energetic forms. According to the Big Bang theory, if the universe were approximately 14 billion years old, this original energy should now be stretched out to around 2 millimeters in the form of microwave radiation.

A friend of Penzias, Bernard Burke, professor of physics at MIT, read a preprint paper by Peebles on the possibility of finding remnant radiation. Burke recognized that Penzias and Wilson discovered what Dicke, Peebles, and Wilkinson were looking for. He told Penzias about this paper and the two groups of scientists eventually got together. The rest is science history.

Penzias and Wilson were not looking for this particular energy, which clearly demonstrates objectivity. They had no intentions of data tampering. Also, this eliminates the possibility that the scientists are experiencing confirmation bias. This discovery caused the scientific community to finally embrace the Big Bang theory. If you stretch out your hand, you can feel this 2-millimeter energy. Well, not really. You can only feel infrared radiation (heat energy), but if you could feel microwave energy, then you would be able to feel it.

# Chapter 7 - Believing Evolution *vs.* Knowing Evolution

*Minds are like parachutes. They only function when they are open.*
-Sir James Dewar (1877-1925)

Robert Riggins in his article, *Do You Believe in Evolution?* (2002), comments upon this particular question, "Do you believe in evolution? It's easy to say "Yes!" but that's not right. The problem is that the question itself is wrong. It's like the old "Have you stopped beating your wife?" question: either a yes or a no give the wrong impression.... The problem is the phrase "believe in"... is the trap.... The phrase believe in, in common parlance seems to mean to take something literally for which there is *little or no objective evidence.*"

This is precisely the reason why many evolutionary biologists will not give a yes or no answer to this particular question. It suggests that they have accepted biological evolution regardless of the physical evidence. Recall that the scientific process filters out claims based upon conjecture. Conforming to the evidence is everything. The goal is to *know* evolution in order to discover the truth. When someone says to me that they do not believe in evolution, I usually follow up with the question, "Well, what is evolution?" Never have I received a correct answer, which tells me that their belief (or disbelief in this case) comes not from their head but from their heart. In effect, someone is disagreeing with something that they have no idea what they are disagreeing about.

The word, evolution, has been connected with evil so often in anti-evolution literature that many Christians cannot even say it without feeling a sense of revulsion. Before one can understand what biological evolution actually is, one must open their mind and honestly listen to the facts. The problem for truth's sake is that this does not have to occur, since it has little bearing upon a happy and fruitful Christian life. In my opinion, though, there is a serious side effect. Not believing in evolution with the understanding that the scientific community has wholeheartedly accepted it creates a lack of trust in how science discovers the truth. Broader problems have arisen because of a lack of trust in the scientific process, such as using alternative sources for their scientific information. This creates scientific illiteracy, or ignorance. Surveys suggest that over 95% of Americans are scientifically illiterate. This produces uninformed political decisions that affect everyone. Dr. Carl Sagan, in his book *The Demon-Haunted World*, does an excellent job of explaining the dangers of scientific illiteracy:

"...consequences of scientific illiteracy are far more dangerous in our time than in any that has come before. It's perilous and foolhardy for the average citizen to remain ignorant about global warming, say, or ozone depletion, air pollution, toxic and radioactive wastes, acid rain, topsoil erosion, tropical deforestation, and exponential population growth. Jobs and wages depend on science and technology. If our nation can't manufacture, at high quality and low price, products people want to buy, then industries will continue to drift away and transfer a little more prosperity to other parts of the world. Consider the social ramifications of fission and fusion power, supercomputers, data "highways," abortion, radon, massive reductions in strategic weapons, addiction, government eavesdropping on the lives of its citizens, high-resolution TV, airline and airport safety, fetal tissue transplants, health costs, food additives, drugs to ameliorate mania or depression or schizophrenia, animal rights, superconductivity, morning-after pills, alleged hereditary antisocial predispositions, space stations, going to Mars, finding cures for AIDS and cancer."
(p. 6 & 7)

I have also noticed that most people who do believe in evolution have similar misconceptions. Because of this, believers for and against evolution can be easily swayed by well-crafted deceptive arguments exploiting common misconceptions. An excellent example of this is with a story about Charles Darwin recanting his belief of evolution on his deathbed. Darwin actually did not renounce his support for evolution and the probable source of this false story is a book written in 1916 called *Bombay Guardian* by H. Enoch. Enoch states that a Protestant fundamentalist, named Lady Hope, claimed to have visited Darwin on his deathbed and that Darwin renounced evolution and accepted Christ. Darwin's daughter, Henrietta, who was with him during his last few days, said Lady Hope never visited Darwin. Even if Charles Darwin did recant his support for evolution on his deathbed, this would have no impact upon why the scientific community supports evolution. Evolutionary theory is not based upon authority-based evidence even from Charles Darwin himself, but is based upon empirical evidence.

It is not surprising that so many people misunderstand evolution. Most dictionaries have incorrect definitions of evolution. For example, Webster's dictionary states: "Evolution – the development of a species, organism, or organ from its original or primitive state to its present or specialized state; phylogeny or ontogeny." Chambers dictionary states: Evolution – the doctrine according to which higher forms of life have gradually arisen out of lower..." Both of these definitions are wrong.

## Biological Evolution

*Evolution* simply means, *change through time*. For example, the English language has changed considerably since the Middle Ages. It has evolved. The body style of the Corvette has changed throughout the years. It also has evolved. Biological evolution deals with life. Contrary to popular belief, Charles Darwin deliberately avoided using the term, evolution. The word is not found in the first five editions of *Origin of Species*, and it is mentioned only once in the sixth edition in an abbreviated form ("evolved"). In Darwin's time, evolution implied a change from an inferior form to a more advanced, or superior form, and Darwin tried to avoid this misconception. He referred to biological evolution as "descent with modification", but even this is no longer considered the most useful definition for scientific research.

It might be good to first know what biological evolution is not. Humans change physically through time from a baby to a full size adult, but this is not considered biological evolution (this is called ontogeny). Caucasians have increased in size in the last thousand years, but this is also not considered biological evolution (the cause is a change in diet). Biological evolution deals with hereditary changes passed on from one generation to the next.

Modern biologists now have a more useful definition in scientific research thanks to discoveries made in genetics. Biologists, Helena Curtis and N. Sue Barnes, define biological evolution as:

"…any change in the frequency of alleles in a gene pool of a population over time."

To better understand this definition, we need to know what DNA, alleles, genes, genomes, and gene pools are. DNA is the hereditary molecule that gets passed on from one generation to the next. It is a blueprint for what we look like and how our bodies operate. The DNA molecule is like a spiral staircase of atoms, and each individual step is called a nucleotide. There are about three billion nucleotides in the DNA molecule. The part of the DNA molecule in the nucleotide that carries the hereditary material is called the nitrogenous base, or *base* for short. There are only four bases, abbreviated as A, C, G, and T. These bases come in twos, where A matches with T and C matches with G. AT and CG are called base pairs.

The DNA molecule is packaged together in a form called a chromosome, and these chromosomes are paired up. Humans have 46 total chromosomes with 23 coming from each parent, which means we have 23 pairs of chromosomes. Any organism that has chromosomes coming in pairs is considered a *diploid* organism.

A gene is a section of the DNA molecule that makes up a hereditary unit unique to one particular characteristic, such as eye color or hair color. The average sized gene in our DNA molecule is about 20,000 base pairs long. For humans, our 46 chromosomes make up approximately 25,000 genes. All of the chromosome information put together is called our genotype. Another way of saying it is our genotype is the sum total of all our genes. When we look at a species as a whole, a characteristic genotype is commonly called a genome, such as the human genome or the chimpanzee genome. Metaphorically speaking, if base pairs were letters, genes would be the sentences, chromosomes would be the chapters, and our genotype would be the whole builders manual. Our sex chapters are our X- and Y-chromosomes.

Diploid organisms, such as human beings, have a maximum of two versions of the same gene (one on each chromosome). Generally, there is a dominant gene and a recessive gene. The dominant gene is usually the one used to build our body, while the recessive gene is not. For example, if you have a gene for brown eyes (dominant) and a gene for blue eyes (recessive), then you will end up with brown eyes. The brown eye gene is expressed, since you have brown eyes. Sometimes both genes are recessive. In this case, the recessive blue eyes will then be expressed, which means the person will have blue eyes.

Just as a genotype is the sum total of all genes in an individual, a *gene pool* is the sum total of all genes in an entire population of organisms or in a species. An individual genome can only have a maximum of two versions of the same gene (one on each chromosome), but a gene pool can have a large number of the same gene. Geneticists have calculated that the average number of versions for each gene within a species is about forty. Each version of a specific gene is called a polymorph, as long as it makes up more than 1% of that particular gene in a gene pool. Some gene pools in animals have over ninety different polymorphs. We can see this variation even in our own species. We have four-foot tall humans and we have seven-foot tall humans. We come in different sizes, shapes, and colors.

What causes there to be so many different variations of the same gene? The biggest cause is mutation. Mutation is a small mistake in the copying of the DNA molecule. It may change base pairs, eliminate base pairs, or even duplicate them (called INDELs). Since the DNA molecule is billions of atoms long, there is bound to be some mistakes made. For example, most mammals have a vitamin C gene, which allows their bodies to make vitamin C. Professors Ohta and Nishikimi from Wakayama Medical University in Wakayama, Japan, have located this vitamin C gene in the DNA molecule in all mammals. Human beings cannot make vitamin C, which is why we need to get it from foods that have vitamin C. Why can't humans make vitamin C? Ohta and Nishikimi discovered a corruption, *i.e.,* a mutation, in the center of the human vitamin C gene. The gene does not work.

Scientists have discovered that most mutations have either no effect upon an organism or they have a negative effect (such as in the case of the vitamin C corruption). Occasionally, a mutation can have a beneficial effect, and possibly help create a new polymorph in the gene pool. For example, in the mid-twentieth century, DDT was used as a pesticide to kill mosquitoes. Originally, it killed almost all of the mosquitoes. Within the mosquito gene pool there existed a DDT-resistant mutation/gene. Today's generation of mosquitoes came from those DDT-resistant individuals, so DDT is no longer effective. This DDT-resistant mutation became beneficial for the mosquito species, and changed in frequency from less that 1% within the gene pool to a very high percentage. When this DDT-resistant gene was in less than 1% of the individuals, it was called a mutation. Once it increased in percentage within the species (thanks to DDT killing the others), the mutation changed its name to a polymorph. This increased variation within the mosquito gene pool.

After thousands of generations, beneficial mutations can accumulate and increase the variation within a population, which increases the size of the gene pool. Other genetic mechanisms, such as recombination, can reshuffle the new genes with the others to create even more variations. The rate of mutation in organisms has been discovered, although it varies between species. The average rate of mutation is about $2.2 \times 10^{-8}$ mutations per base pair per generation. This means that we have about one hundred mutation-induced changes within our genome that we did not inherit from our parents. Mutation rate is important for biologists to know, because it puts a limit on how fast evolution can occur. Since evolution needs multiple versions of genes to select from, the overall rate of evolution will be proportionally lower in species with lower variation.

*Alleles* are different versions of the same gene. For example, the hanging ear lobe gene is one allele in the human gene pool, while the attached ear lobe gene is another allele of that particular gene. When a population of organisms has a higher concentration of one allele over another, then this allele is said to have a higher frequency within that gene pool. In human beings, 70% - 90 % of us have the hanging ear lobe allele, which means that the hanging ear lobe allele is present at a high frequency in the human gene pool.

If after a thousand generations we notice that the percent of human beings with hanging ear lobes is down to 20%, then the frequency of hanging ear lobe alleles has changed. This would be considered biological evolution, since there was a *change in the frequency of alleles in a gene pool of a population over time.* Recall that the frequency of DDT-resistant alleles changed within the mosquito gene pool, so according to the definition of biological evolution, mosquitoes have evolved within just a few generations.

## Mechanisms of Evolution

What causes a change in the frequency of alleles within a gene pool from generation to generation? The answer to this is what made Charles Darwin so famous. Darwin did not come up with the idea of evolution. That occurred over 2,000 years earlier with an Ionian Greek named Anaximander of Miletus. Darwin discovered the primary reason how populations evolve, and he called it natural selection.

Changes in the environment can cause certain expressed variations to be favored over others as one generation reproduces into the next. This is called natural selective pressure. For example, if a local environment suddenly experienced a long-term climate change from grassland to desert and a camel-like mammal population inhabited this location, then this population must either adapt to the change, move, or perish. Those that stay would be forced to adapt to a drier climate.

Thanks to variations of alleles within the gene pool of this camel-like population, some individuals can endure longer periods without water than others. The more "desert-proof" individuals have a much better chance of surviving travels between water holes than the more "desert-prone" individuals. The desert-proof individuals are undergoing less stress than their counterparts, thereby increasing their chances of doing the mating and producing offspring for the next generation. The next generation of camels will have a higher frequency of the desert-proof alleles, since most of their parents were desert-proof individuals. In other words, the process of natural selection has caused the species to evolve. This also means that the next generation has a greater chance of survival in a drier climate than the previous generation.

Natural selection is not evolution; it is a mechanism for evolution to occur. There are other mechanisms that can cause evolution, such as sexual selection and genetic drift. Sexual selection is a type of natural selection specific to reproductive success. For example, the peacock's huge tail actually increases the chance for it to be caught by a predator, but females have a preference for huge tail displays. This sexual selective pressure outweighs the natural selective pressure of predation, which ensures that large tails get passed onto successive generations (as long as too many of them do not get killed by predators).

Genetic drift is a random change in the frequency of alleles in a gene pool. An example of this is when a small population invades a new territory, such as a small flock of birds landing on an isolated island and gets permanently separated from the rest of the population. The small gene pool in this flock does not perfectly represent the larger gene pool of the original population. Some genetic variations are not represented within the smaller flock. The frequency of alleles in the new gene pool is different at the very onset of separation. The small population will now undergo different mutations and different selective pressures. This is called the *founder effect*. It is relatively easy for geneticists to identify species that have gone through a recent founder effect, because their genotype will show a dramatically reduced number of genetic variations (fewer polymorphs).

## Speciation and Common Ancestry

When most people say they do not believe in evolution, it is not really biological evolution that they are challenging; it is the historical aspect of evolution. It is the evolutionary change in organisms throughout the history of life that is the real issue. Terms scientists use when they deal with evolutionary change through time are speciation and common ancestry.

*Speciation* is when one species gives rise to one or more additional species. A species can be defined as a group of organisms that are reproductively isolated from any other. Two populations of a particular species may not be able to breed with each other because of geographic isolation (trapped on an island) or behavioral reasons (a change in mating season). As the generations progress, each population will experience different heritable changes in their ever changing gene pool thanks to mutation and evolution. Eventually, each group will become so different that they can no longer breed successfully even if they tried. This can be seen with the horse and the donkey. Their gene pools have diverged to such an extent that their offspring, the mule, cannot successfully breed. In the future, as heritable changes continue and their gene pools further diverge, interbreeding will produce no offspring.

*Common ancestry* is a genealogical view of the diversity of life, such as you and your cousins having a common grandfather. Grandpa is the common ancestor to all of you. When biologists say two separate species have a common ancestor, they mean that there have been successive heritable changes in these two separate populations since they became isolated in the past.

Species that are closely related to each other share a recent common ancestor, while species more distantly related share a more distant ancestor. All horse-like mammals share a horse-like ancestor. All hoofed mammals, such as horses and rhinos, share an even more distant common ancestor. All mammals of any type share an even further distant ancestor. This is the area where many have such a difficult time with Charles Darwin, because he explained that by going back in time even further all organisms on the planet, including human beings, share a distant single-celled common ancestor.

A good analogy for common ancestry is the bush or tree, where the trunk represents the ancient common ancestor of all organisms and each branch represents a particular class of organisms, such as ancient mammals, reptiles, and amphibians. Branching off from these are families of organisms, like ancient cats, bears, and canines on the mammal branch. All living organisms are represented at the very tips of each limb.

## Misconceptions about Evolution

Why are there so many misconceptions about evolution? Although, the basic idea of biological evolution is simple, understanding the details is an exercise in thought. This requires an exertion of mental energy, which takes time. The following are common misconceptions about biological evolution that are promoted by anti-evolution creationists.

### Misconception 1: "Evolution says that we came from monkeys. This is impossible, because monkeys are still around today."

This statement is incorrect for a number of reasons. First, it suggests that evolutionary scientists claim human beings evolved from monkeys. This is not correct. If this seems unbelievable, then research all of the peer-reviewed literature on biological evolution. You will find that no one promoting this. Monkeys are creatures that live today. Modern monkeys did not exist millions of years ago, so it would be impossible for humans to evolve from them. Nowhere do scientists suggest that humans evolved from any other *living* organism. Although, scientists do accept that all primates, i.e., humans, apes, monkeys, lemurs, and tarsiers, share a common primate ancestor.

The second reason why the "we came from monkeys" statement is incorrect is because it insinuates evolution is a process by which higher forms of animals gradually arise from lower forms. This is what Charles Darwin attempted to avoid by not using the word evolution in his published works. Evolution merely acts upon populations adapting to changes in their local environments. There is no evolutionary goal to become a higher organism. There are many examples of organisms evolving to what is considered a lower form. For example, certain animals that have adapted to caves now have useless eyes. Sight is useless in caves, so there is no need for eyes. A population evolving to a blind state is contrary to arising from a lower form.

Thirdly, the "this is impossible, because monkeys are still around today" phrase demonstrates a critical misunderstanding of the evolutionary process. It suggests that as one species (the parent species) evolves into a new species (the daughter species), the parent species dies out. This is an old and discredited view of evolution, where a ladder or a chain represents evolutionary change from one species to the next. An evolutionary ladder suggests that a daughter species is one rung higher and replaces a more primitive parent species. An evolutionary chain metaphor creates the same idea, where the daughter species is one link higher. Remnants of this discredited idea can be seen when someone in the popular press claims a scientists has discovered a missing link.

Using the more appropriate branching tree metaphor, one can see that a separate daughter species CAN exist at the same time as a parent species, since a new species merely branches off. The original branch may still exist, or it just might wither off. This demonstrates that no living species is higher on any evolutionary ladder than any other living species. Humans and chimpanzees are both modern creatures. Also, there is no such thing as a "missing link", since the link metaphor is an incorrect representation of the evolutionary process.

**Misconception 2: "It is statistically impossible for complex organs to evolve by chance?"**

Anti-evolution creationists are constantly telling their Christian audiences that evolution is statistical impossible. They start out by saying that evolution proceeds by chance only, and then explain that it is a mathematical improbability for any complex biological system to evolve from simple organic molecules. They then say that it is more mathematically probable for a 747 jet to be assembled from scrap metal in a junkyard by the winds of a tornado than for evolution to occur by chance. This logic is quite convincing, but it has a fatal flaw.

Evolution does not proceed by chance at all, but by selective mechanisms, such as natural selection, genetic drift, and gene flow. Chance enters into the equation due to the randomness of mutation, which produces variability in the gene pool. *Evolution uses the mutation rate; it is not guided by it.*

Also, whether a mutation will occur or not is not governed by chance, either. Remember, each generation will have over 100 additional mutations than the previous generation. Even though mutations are a random process, variability is a certainty. Chance only comes into play as to what kind of mutation is going to occur and when.

Another reason why "chance" is so threatening to anti-evolution creationists is because they argue that it is taking God out of the picture. "If we are the product of mere chance, then God was not involved and does not exist." From a Christian perspective, allowing chance to occur is evidence for God's gift of free will as I will discuss in further detail in the last chapter. Pure chance in the natural world can be just another divine tool in the creation toolbox for God.

**Misconception 3: "Something irreducibly complex could not have evolved"**

The irreducible complexity argument goes like this, "Each stage in evolution must be an improvement from the previous stage in order for there to be a selective advantage. A complex organ, like an ear, requires multiple parts working together in order to function. A reduction of any one part makes it a useless organ. Any earlier evolutionary stage, like a quarter of an ear or a half an ear, does not work. How can a useless half an ear be an improvement over a useless quarter of an ear? If the next stage is just as useless as the previous stage, then there is no selective advantage and it will not evolve into a complex part."

This kind of argument preys upon people's misconceptions of the evolutionary process. First, it incorrectly assumes that evolution requires each stage to be an improvement upon the previous stage with the goal of creating a complex organ, such as the ear or the eye. There is no goal of evolution to create any improved or complex part. Evolution is a product of a population adapting to its current environment. If this requires a reduction in complexity, then a reduction will occur. As stated earlier, this is seen with animals trapped in a cave for many generations. Their eyes become useless.

Second, it incorrectly assumes that each component part of a complex organ, such as the tiny malleus, incus, and stapes bones of the middle ear, has always had only one function (hearing), which has never changed. If this were the case, then it would be highly unlikely for complex organs to evolve. Most organs or parts of organs have more than one function. This is called *co-opting*. For example, the nose is used for smelling AND breathing. Evolution modifies individual features by taking advantage of components having overlapping functions.

Third, this argument incorrectly assumes that each successive stage in evolution of a complex multi-component organ, like the ear, is a matter of adding another component part. This is not the case at all. Evolution works upon what is available. It never "creates" a new part from nothing. As individual features become modified upon successive generations, new secondary functions may arise while the primary functions are still being performed. Eventually, the secondary function may change into the primary function. This ensures that there will be a next stage of evolution, even though there is no goal of a complex organ.

### The Evolution of Hearing in Mammals

An example of a prominent creationist misrepresenting how individual features can evolve to form a complex system is Duane Gish. Gish, a non-practicing biologist, wrote a book on fossils called *Evolution: The Fossils Say No!*. Nowhere in his formal education or his published research has he any experience in paleontology, but that did not stop him from writing this book. The problem is that his lack of experience in this field has created fatal errors in his logic. The following quote is Gish commenting upon how it is impossible for mammals to evolve from reptiles, as evolutionary theory states.

"All mammals, living or fossil, have a single bone, the dentary, on each side of the lower jaw, and all mammals, living or fossil, have three auditory ossicles or ear bones, the malleus, incus and stapes.... Every reptile, living or fossil, however, has at least four bones in the lower jaw and only one auditory ossicle, the stapes.... There are no transitional fossil forms showing, for instance, three or two jawbones, or two ear bones. No one has explained yet, for that matter, how the transitional form would have managed to chew while his jaw was being unhinged and rearticulated, or how he would hear while dragging two of his jaw bones up into his ear."

Gish incorrectly assumes that each feature (bones in this case) only has one function. Gish makes the comment about transitional fossils that have two jawbones or two ear bones, because he is ignoring the possibility of overlapping functions, or co-opting, with the bones in question. Just as we feel the vibrations of a bowling ball dropping on the floor, the jaws of bottom-dwelling fish, amphibians, and reptiles can feel vibrations with their lower jaws, because their jaws are in contact with the ground. As a predator gets closer, the vibrations get stronger, which clues them in to evading. Notice the lower jaw has two functions, one for biting and the other for "hearing" vibrations. Coincidentally, these are the jawbones that transitioned to hearing bones in the mammal line.

Gish claims that there are no intermediate fossils that show this transition. This is nothing less than an act of deceiving his readers. There are four bones involved in this jaw-ear transition as the mammal line evolved from a specific reptile line. Reptiles have one earbone, the stapes, and three lower jawbones, the quadrate, the articular, and the dentary. Mammals have three earbones, the stapes, the incus (quadrate), and the malleus (articular), and one jawbone, the dentary. All four bones are in contact with each other in both the reptiles and the mammals. In the fossil record, there are extinct creatures known as mammal-like reptiles that show a detailed transition from the two reptile jawbones, the quadrate and the articular, transitioning in size and position into the two mammal earbones, the incus and the malleus.

The most primitive mammal-like reptiles, the *pelycosaurs* (about 270 million years ago), had the reptile jaw-ear setup. The later *therapsid* mammal-like reptiles (about 250 million years ago) also have the reptile setup, but the quadrate and the articular bone show mammalian characteristics of becoming earbones. The later *cynodonts* (about 240 million years ago) show the mammalian dentary-only jawbone, which means the quadrate and articular bones are primarily earbones. They have the mammal jaw-ear setup, but showing reptile characteristics. The *morganucodontid* cynodont-mammals (about 190 million years ago) show an even more mammal jaw-ear setup.

Even though the fossil record does an excellent job of corroborating evolutionary co-opting to show how complex organs can evolve, intelligent design proponents say there are certain examples where it is physically impossible. It is only physically impossible in the mind of the intelligent design proponent claiming impossibility. In every case, a plausible evolutionary pathway has been given.

### The Evolution of Flight in Birds

Another example of a prominent creationist misrepresenting the evolutionary process pertaining to complex organs is Walt Brown, author of *In the Beginning: Compelling Evidence for Creation and the Flood*. In his book, he makes the assumption that in order for a wing to evolve from a leg it must go through a half a wing stage:

"What use is half a wing? A leg evolving into a wing would be a bad leg long before it was a good wing."

With the recent discoveries of some small dinosaur fossils that show feathers and a fercula (wish bone), the scientific community has generally accepted that birds evolved from bipedal (two legs and two arms) dinosaurs and not quadrupedal (four legs) reptiles. In view of this, the first error in Brown's comment is that the bird's wing has its origins in a freely moving arm rather than a walking leg.

Brown has also succumbed to the same evolutionary misconceptions as Gish did. He has assumed that features, such as the arm and the wing in this case, have only one function. Overlapping functions of the feather and the arm make the evolution of the wing through co-opting highly plausible. The following is a possible history of how the bird's wing evolved from the dinosaur's arm from a perspective of evading a predator. This scenario might not be the actual history, but it does show that the evolution of the bird's wing is quite possible. To further demonstrate the relatively high probability of wings evolving in a population of down-covered dinosaurs, I will present a second possible evolutionary pathway, an aquatic one.

In the late Triassic or Early Jurassic Period, there were small bipedal dinosaurs covered with down. Down is just another version of feathers. Just as in today's birds, the down probably had a primary function of insulation, especially since fast moving dinosaurs were most likely warm-blooded. Many of today's birds have beautiful plumage thanks to an evolutionary process called sexual selection. The males put on a display for the females in order to successfully mate with them. This can be seen with the peacock and its huge tail feathers. After many generations, the feathers have become extremely modified, just because the preferred males had the best chance of passing on their genes to the next generation.

The modification of down into feathers on arms for display may also have come about by challenging male rivals, as some species of birds do today. The larger the arm feathers and the more motion the arms create, the more intimidating it would be to other males. This would also improve the chances that these males successfully pass on their genes (and the improved display features) to the next generation. The early down covered dinosaurs could have participated in sexual display, which occurs in their descendents, the birds. As the down on the arms became larger through sexual selection, new functions had the opportunity to arise.

Today, chickens escape from predators by first running. When the predator gets close enough to bite, chickens change tactics and flap their wings and fly to safety. If in a population of ancient small down covered dinosaurs an individual genetically acquired the skill of flapping its feathered arms at the point of attack (resulting in a more effective evasion tactic), this individual will have had a better chance of surviving and pass on its genes to the next generation. After many generations, more individuals will have inherited this skill. Eventually, this characteristic would get more pronounced since distance away from a predator equates to increased chances of survival. The flapping of the wings for a short thrust of flight will eventually lead to efficient flight.

There is a possible aquatic natural selection process that could have caused flight in birds, especially since one of the earliest birds discovered in the fossil record is very duck-like. If a population of down covered dinosaurs found success in floating on water like modern day ducks, then this could open the way for flight. If the population began using an evading technique of running on water (especially having webbed feet), then this would improve an individual's chances for survival. After a number of generations, all of the individuals in the population would be using this technique. Taking this one step further, if an individual accelerated its evasion speed of running on water in order to increase distance by flapping its feathered arms, then this would improve its chances for success. The next generations would probably benefit from the flapping assisted running. Eventually, this would transition into short flights from one side of the lake to the other.

Both scenarios may not have occurred at all, but they are plausible and are supported by empirical evidence. What this does show is that complex features, such as the wings of birds or the hearing of mammals, are not irreducibly complex.

**Misconception 4: "Scientists are beginning to question the validity of evolution"**

This is a common claim by many creationists, but it is just plain wrong. This can easily be tested. Look up all of the peer-reviewed scientific literature on evolution in the past twenty years. It is available to the public in libraries across America and is now becoming available online. If scientists were beginning to question the validity of evolution, then there should be an increased amount of articles in these peer-reviewed scientific journals that show scientists questioning it. Peer-reviewed literature is the way scientists communicate any scientific research.

I can save you the trip to the library or search on the internet. There are a total of zero articles of scientists questioning the validity of evolution among the thousands of articles published on evolution.

**Misconception 5: "Evolution is based upon nothing but conjecture."**

I hear many times anti-evolution creationists tout the claim that evolution is based upon nothing but wild conjecture. I would like to challenge this claim with empirical evidence. According to Webster's dictionary, the definition of conjecture is "an opinion that is not supported by evidence". If these anti-evolution creationists are correct, then there should be no empirical evidence that supports evolution, regardless if it is correct or not. The following is an incomplete list of some empirical evidence that supports evolutionary theory.

**Biological evolution has been observed (an empirical fact)**

This is not disputed by anti-evolution creationists, because of the requirement of the ark animals undergoing rapid evolution in order to create the ten million plus species of today. The point here is that if all life did evolve from a common ancestor, then we would see the natural mechanisms in place causing evolution today, and we do. This is an additional piece of evidence supporting common ancestry.

**The diversity of today's life fits into evolutionary categories**

The patterns of relatedness between living species conform to the patterns expected if all life evolved from a common ancestor. We should have categories of single-celled organisms, fish, amphibians, reptiles, birds, mammals, *etc.* Today's diversity of life are not diverse from each other, but are genetically connected.

**The fossil record matches common ancestry**

The pattern of fossils in the sedimentary rocks is identical to what should be expected if all organisms evolved from a common ancestor. In the deepest layers there are no fossils, since life did not exist during the early formation of Earth. Single-celled fossils are found in layers just above these. Fossils of simple multi-celled organisms are then discovered followed by progressively more complex and diverse fossils as the rock layers get younger. Also, intermediate organisms, such as the fish-like amphibians, amphibian-like reptiles, mammal-like reptiles, dog-like bears, bird-like dinosaurs, *etc.,* are found in the appropriate aged rock layers. Lastly, 98% of all fossils are of extinct organisms. This pattern in the fossil record also conforms to common ancestry. As environmental stresses change, organisms will either evolve or go extinct, ultimately resulting in species change.

## Genetics matches evolution

Prior to genetics, patterns of relatedness between living species had already been established by comparing physical features. For example, all primates (humans, apes, monkeys, lemurs, etc.) have fingernails and have relatively large brains. Using physical comparisons, a pattern of common ancestry with all living organisms was created. DNA is the blueprint for all of life. If all of life is genetically related, i.e., descended from a common ancestor, then these blue prints should be similar. Also, just as children look more similar to their parents and less so to their grandparents, DNA in more closely related species should be more similar to each other than distantly related species. This is exactly the case. For example, it has been known that the great apes were the closest ancestors to human beings because of physical characteristics. Genetics has shown that humans and chimpanzees are 98.6% identical, while gorillas are 96% identical to humans. Additionally, chimps are genetically closer to humans than they are to gorillas.

Also, the discoveries of genes that are turned off in living organisms suggest evolutionary stages that the species went through. Humans have the genes for gills and a tail. Dolphins have the genes for nose smelling (smelling does not work in the water). Horses have genes for toes. Birds have genes for hand claws and reptilian body scales.

## Comparative anatomy conforms to evolutionary theory

The fin of a dolphin, the wing of a bat, the hand of a human, and the front foot of a bear all share the same bones in their front appendage, but all have different primary functions. If all life did evolve from a common ancestor, then this is exactly the pattern that we should see. All of these organisms are mammals, which have a common mammal ancestor that possessed a front foot appendage.

**Evolution predicts vestigial features on living organisms**

Common ancestry predicts that living organisms and extinct fossils should show vestiges of their evolutionary past. The following are some examples. Human beings have wisdom teeth (back molars) that do not fit, ear-wiggling muscles, a remnant third eyelid (nictitating membrane), deep canine roots, and goose bumps. Pigs have hanging toes on their back legs. Whales and boas have hips (hips are designed to support legs).

**Ontogeny**

As embryos develop they go through remnant stages as relic genes get turned off. Human embryos go through a stage with gills and a tail. Horses go through a stage of having toes. Birds go through a stage with hand claws.

**Ativism**

If remnant genes do not get turned off, then they just might get expressed. Some human babies are born with tails that get surgically removed. Julius Caesar's horse had toes. Sometimes whales are caught that possess small legs.

Each of these categories has many more examples, which is additional empirical evidence. Even if all of this evidence is not convincing enough, the unavoidable conclusion is that evolution is not based upon conjecture.

## Misconception 6: "Macroevolution violates God's Word."

It is very clear reading anti-evolution creationist literature that even though they accept evolution within kinds they overwhelmingly deny evolution between kinds, which they call macroevolution. Why? As stated earlier, they interpret, "according to their kind", in the Book of Genesis as to mean God created all of life and placed them into preset divine categories, such as a whale category. The actual Hebrew word for kind is *baramin*. Any claim stating that modern species evolved from different "kinds" of animals, such as today's whales being descended from a land mammal with legs cannot be compatible with their literal interpretation of the Bible.

What is the accepted definition of macroevolution within the scientific community? They rarely use the term, macroevolution, but generally they consider it a historical look at evolutionary change at the species level or higher. It has been stated that microevolution is evolution within a species, while macroevolution is evolution between species.

As stated earlier, anti-evolution creationists have a different definition of macroevolution, because they are connecting it to the biblical term, *baramin*. *Baramin* does not equate to species. The horse kind category is not a species level category, but it is a family level category. What does family level mean? Scientists have organized all of life into progressively more specific categories based upon levels of relatedness. For example, the classification system organizes horses as follows: Kingdom – *Animalia* (all animals), Phylum – *Chordata* (all animals with spinal cords), Class – *Mammalia* (all mammals), Order – *Perissodactyla* (all odd-toed mammals such as horses, rhinos, and tapirs), Family – *Equidae* (horses, asses, and zebras), Genus – *Equus* (all horses), Species – *caballus* (a species of horse). Since horses, asses, and zebras are very horse-like, then this is probably what God meant by kind.

Most creationists claim that the Book of Genesis excludes the possibility of macroevolution, which comes from their belief that *baramin*, or kind, is a divine preset and permanent category of organism. The following are the specific verses in Genesis that use the phrase, "after his kind":

-(Genesis 1:12): "And the earth brought forth grass, and herb yielding seed after his kind, and the tree yielding fruit, whose seed was in itself, after his kind: and God saw that it was good."

-(Genesis 1:21): "And God created great whales, and every living creature that moveth, which the waters brought forth abundantly, after their kind, and every winged fowl after his kind: and God saw that it was good."

-(Genesis 1:24): "And God said, Let the earth bring forth the living creature after his kind, cattle, and creeping thing, and beast of the earth after his kind: and it was so."

-(Genesis 1:25): "And God made the beast of the earth after his kind, and cattle after their kind, and every thing that creepeth upon the earth after his kind: and God saw that it was good."

-(Genesis 7:14,15): "They, and every beast after his kind, and all the cattle after their kind, and every creeping thing that creepeth upon the earth after his kind, and every fowl after his kind, every bird of every sort. And they went in unto Noah into the ark, two and two of all flesh, wherein is the breath of life."

In their opinion, "after his kind" conflicts with the evolutionary concept of common ancestry, which states that all living organisms are descended from a common ancient ancestor. On the surface, it looks like common ancestry conforms to the creationists' definition of macroevolution (evolution between kinds), thus conflicting with their interpretation of the phrase, "after their kind". Little do most Christians realize, common ancestry is NOT evolution between kinds, which means it does not conform to the creationists' definition of macroevolution. Common ancestry actually conforms to their definition of microevolution, which they accept. The idea that all organisms have a common ancestor is actually evolution WITHIN kinds, regardless of the definition of kinds.

If common ancestry states that the ancestor to all mammals was a non-mammal, i.e., an ancient reptile species, then how can this not be the creationists' definition macroevolution? The answer is that evolution acts strictly upon populations from one generation to the next, which means that all modern mammals descended from their own kind, their parents. It has nothing to do with what happened 10,000 or 100,000 generations ago, or what is going to happen in the far future.

The divine category of kind can be restated in terms of genetics as the overall genetic makeup, *i.e., the combined gene pools of all the species within that kind.* For example, most creation scientists agree that giraffes are a kind of animal. Today there are a number of giraffe species, but they all look like giraffes. Most artist reconstructions of Noah and the ark tend to have two giraffes either walking into the ark or they have their long necks sticking out of the roof. Genetic mutations (about 100 new mutations per individual) guarantee that the next generation of giraffe kind will have a slightly different set of alleles than the previous one. Notice how the definition of kind must be flexible enough to take into account additional new variations upon each successive generation. *This shows that the kind categories are not fixed categories.* Subtle changes in the total number and version of alleles from one generation to the next causes the category to change slightly.

Common ancestry claims that all mammals have a common ancestor, which means that modern day giraffes must have descended from mammals that had shorter necks. The fossil record confirms this with progressively older rocks containing giraffe-like mammals with progressively shorter necks. The oldest giraffe-like fossils are very deer-like in their morphology.

Besides having shorter necks, the most primitive giraffe-like fossils look deer-like. This also conforms to common ancestry, since giraffes are genetically similar to the deer family. Today, the giraffe and the deer are very distinct from each other, but it gets very difficult to separate them in the fossil record. The problem for many creationists is that deer are a different kind than giraffes. Common ancestry is conflicting with their definition of macroevolution. A certain population did not directly evolve from one set kind (deer) into another (giraffe), the kind evolved with it. The category of giraffe kind did not exist at the time of *Eumeryx*. More importantly, this does not conflict with the Book of Genesis, since each population of mammals is living and breeding after their kind at the time of their kind. This particular ancient population of deer-like mammals progressively changed their overall genetic makeup (kind) through time, yet they stayed true to after their kind and still do.

Organisms do not evolve from one kind to the next, as defined by anti-evolution creationists' macroevolution. Their kind is inherently part of them, so organisms and their kind category evolve together. Since their kind category changes along with organisms, it guarantees that they always evolve WITHIN, or "after their kind". This means that there is no conflict between common ancestry and Genesis. Interestingly, modern elephants, rhinos, camels, deer, sheep, pigs, horses, and hippos show a similar common ancestry pattern in the fossil record as in the case of the giraffe. Additionally, the ancestors to all of these very distinct kinds of mammals look more similar to each other than they do of their modern descendants.

Those opposed to this view may say that "after his kind" refers to preset categories, thus are not subject to change through time. God created kind categories then filled the categories with all of life. The problem with this interpretation is that it does not match God's other infallible revelation, nature. As stated earlier, the overall variation within a kind category changes with the next generation, so the kind parameters just changed. Taking the Book of Genesis literally, it could just as likely mean that while God is creating separate and distinct organisms, they are conveniently fitting into different categories. The purpose is "separate and distinct", not "must fit into pre-made categories". Once complete, Adam now has the ability to name them since they are different from each other:

> -"And out of the ground the LORD God formed every beast of the field, and every fowl of the air; and brought them unto Adam to see what he would call them: and whatsoever Adam called every living creature, that was the name thereof.
> -And Adam gave names to all cattle, and to the fowl of the air, and to every beast of the field; but for Adam there was not found an help meet for him." (Genesis 2:19,20)

Also, the follow-on assumption that kinds are unchanging through time is not a direct biblical interpretation, but a man-made restriction on God's Word. Nowhere does it say, "kinds are unchanging categories". This is only a best-guess human interpretation in order to fit a specific interpretation. God is merely explaining to the reader that he purposely created life in a variety of forms that are separate and distinct from each other. If we look at the diversity of life at any moment in time in the past, organisms always fit into categories, which do not necessarily have to be today's categories. Today, there are no dinosaurs or mammal-like reptiles, but at the time they existed on earth, they fit into their own categories. During the time of dinosaurs, there were no giraffes, elephants or camels. The biblical fact that organisms have always fit into distinct categories in no way excludes the possibility that all of life had a common ancestor. Defining a kind of organism, whether it is at the species, genus, family, order, class, phylum, or kingdom level only refers to organisms at any one moment in time.

There is another conflict with anti-evolution creationists' interpretation of the phrase "after their kind". Notice that every time the phrase is used in Genesis it refers to organisms that can reproduce with each other. Today, anti-evolution creationists consider kind to mean organisms that sometimes cannot reproduce with each other successfully, such as the chimpanzee and gorilla.

**Misconception 7: "Evolution has occurred, but only by what is called, microevolution."**

Today, almost all anti-evolution creationists accept the scientific definition of biological evolution, although they call it microevolution. They consider microevolution as evolution occurring within kinds of organisms. This is only a recent belief within the anti-evolution creationist community. Up until recently, all anti-evolution creationists zealously rejected any kind of biological evolution, but they soon realized a major problem with their interpretation of events dealing with Noah's flood. It is a big stretch to believe that millions of species of animals, living and extinct (such as all of the dinosaurs), fit into one big ark and survived for one full year. Besides it being a physical impossibility for this many organisms to fit into one ark, how can a handful of people care for millions of species on a daily basis for a full year? The death of one clean animal would spell doom for that species. Also, where could all the food, specific to each species, be stored?

To save their interpretation of Genesis, certain anti-evolution creationists came up with the "kinds" solution. As stated earlier, when God stated, "two of every kind", he did not mean two of every species of animal. He meant two of every category of animal. For example, horses, donkeys, and zebras, make up a kind of horse animal. Wolves, foxes, coyotes, jackals, and dogs make up a kind of canine animal. This means, only one pair of horse kind, dog kind, pig kind, snake kind, etc. entered the ark. Instead of millions of species of animals entering the ark, only hundreds of kinds of animals needed to enter.

This claim then requires that all of these kinds of animals leaving the ark to not only "go forth and multiply and replenish the Earth" but also to evolve at an accelerated rate in order to create today's millions of diverse species. This type of accelerated evolution (rejected by scientists) is what creationists call microevolution. This kinds solution may have solved the room availability problem (at least for believers since it requires only a few correctly placed miracles), but it now has created some physical impossibilities. A closer look at genetics reveals some fatal errors in this anti-evolution creationist claim.

## Ark Animals Paradox

An understanding of how evolution works on different versions of alleles within a population's gene pool reveals a serious problem for the anti-evolution creationists' claim. They claim that ALL of the 10 million-plus species of living (extant) animals are descended from the few animals that were in Noah's ark just a few thousand years ago. As just stated, they realize that an ark, regardless of size, could not possibly fit 10 million species. To overcome this hurdle, they claim that only generalized kinds were on the ark, such as one mouse kind and one horse kind. They then claim that after the waters receded, the generalized kinds diversified and underwent an accelerated post-flood evolution in order to account for the vast number of species we have today.

This accelerated post-flood evolution is a genetic impossibility. If a species is decimated down to two individuals or even seven pairs, it is impossible for that species to evolve (at least until mutation creates new versions of genes, and that would take hundreds of thousands of years based upon known mutation rates). Evolution is a selection process, which means that a species needs multiple variations of a gene to select from. Recall, that the maximum number of alleles a pair of diploid organisms can pass onto the next generation is four, two from each parent. Generally, it will be even less than four alleles if each parent has the same version of a gene. Most genes will become *fixed*, which means that there will be only one version to chose from. Fixed genes can be seen in the Japanese population with eye color. Everyone has brown eyes, because that is the only eye color allele available.

The known mutation rate is much too slow. Mutations occur at an extremely low rate ($2.2 \times 10^{-8}$ per base pair per generation), and most of these are either neutral or negative. Only rarely do beneficial mutations occur resulting in a new allele, and even more rarely do these become expressed. Even if it becomes expressed, very rarely does the allele increase in percentage into the population upon successive generations. Most disappear just as fast as they appear. Mathematically, it would take millions of years to create the diversity of alleles in all of the species around the world even with the assistance of genetic recombination.

The following example should make this clear. Today, there are over 40 million dogs just in the United States alone. The dog gene pool has many variations of any particular allele, and we see this by the many hundreds of breeds of dog. We have Great Danes, German Shepards, Collies, Golden Retrievers, Greyhounds, *etc*. Let us assume that some disease decimated the dog population down to just two poodles. If after successful breeding the population of dogs got back up to 40 million, then we would have 40 million poodles. Great Danes, German Shepherds, Collies, Golden Retrievers, Greyhound, and all of the other breeds would be gone forever.

Not only do anti-evolution creationists believe that evolution occurred where it is physically impossible to occur, they also believe that it occurred at an accelerated rate. This accelerated rate is impossible even with today's variations. In reality, selection of favored traits would not occur until mutations created variability. Since at first the variability is low, evolution would be slow. Once the variability increased throughout successive generations, evolution would also increase. This process is physically impossible in just a few thousand years, and is exactly opposite to what anti-evolution creationists are claiming. Instead of initial accelerated evolution followed by a progressively slower rate to today's rate, it would initially by extremely slow followed by a progressively greater rate.

The only way around the genetics paradox for anti-evolution creationists is to claim that God invoked sets of increasing variation miracles upon each kind. Once a population of kinds increases in numbers, God would then miraculously add multitudes of alleles into each individual genome in order to allow evolution to operate. Nowhere does the Bible hint that this occurred. The origins of this claim were to resolve the implausible idea that Noah had to take care of millions of species. It is not the product of a direct interpretation of a biblical verse.

This claim can be tested. If there was a dramatic increase in evolution rates a few thousand years ago, then physical and historical evidence should show this. There should be no early cave paintings of specialized modern species, but they should show generalized "kind" species. This is not the case. Ancient cave paintings are of ice age megafauna, and these creatures are very specialized. Ancient rock drawings in North Africa are of today's African animals. Also, mummified ancient Egyptian animals, such as cats, should look more like a generalized cat kind that tigers, lions, cheetahs, house cats, cougars, jaguars, leopards, and civets would equally evolve from. The problem is that these mummified cats look identical to modern day house cats.

Here is another test. Everyone agrees that Native Americans populated North and South America thousands of years ago from Asia. Young Earth creationists believe it occurred just after the flood. If the mutation rate was miraculously increased at first, then there should be a large genetic different between Native Americans and their Asian progenitors. This is also not the case. Even with thousands of years of separation, there have been very few genetic changes.

## No New Information Paradox

In an attempt to counter what anti-evolution creationists call macroevolution, they claim that mutations never, or at best, rarely increase genetic information (new alleles). Tim Wallace's young earth creationist website, www.trueorigins.org, has multiple examples and links of anti-evolution creationist experts claiming this.

Little do young earth anti-evolution creationists realize, this claim directly contradicts their other claim that all of today's thirteen (or more) million species micro-evolved from the few animals that left Noah's ark. "Two of every kind" and "seven pairs of every clean animals" can only carry 4 alleles per gene type and 28 alleles per gene type, respectively (each individual can only have 2 alleles maximum per gene). Today, there are 92 different alleles of a particular gene in the common mouse (unclean animal – Leviticus 11:29). That means according to the anti-evolution creationist scenario, 88 alleles of this gene were generated after the flood (four were in the original pair). This is a dramatic increase in information that was not present in the original ark animals. Where did the new alleles come from? Homologous recombination cannot be the answer, because this just reshuffles the four alleles already available. The only answer is beneficial genetic mutation.

Creationist and geneticists Chris Ashcraft confirms this problem, and even admits that most anti-evolution creationists are wrong:

"In spite of this rather overwhelming evidence, most creationists still tend to assume there is no mechanism for generating new genetic information …"

To compound this problem, kinds to an anti-evolution creationist is not at the species level. Lions, tigers, leopards, mountain lions, cheetahs, civets, and the common house cat are all a kind of animal. Different versions of any particular gene now add up in the thousands!

God could have performed multiple genetic miracles upon each post-flood animal, but the act of forcing change is an admission of God's fallibility. Actively altering the future means it was not done right in the first place. There are literal interpretations that do not require any intervention miracles.

With this additional information in mind, the actual anti-evolution creationist definition of microevolution is "...any change in the frequency of alleles in a gene pool of a population over time as to not increase information (new alleles), with the exception of new alleles created though the miraculous intervention of God". The scientific community does not accept this definition of microevolution, because of its internal contradictions and it being useless as a tool to understand nature.

**Misconception 8: "Evolution is not in the Bible"**

One argument presented by some Christians is, "since evolution is not mentioned in the Bible then it did not occur." Absence of evidence must mean evidence of absence. If this type of logic is correct, then Jesus never had a life between ages 12 and 30, since it is not mentioned in the Bible. If one truly understands the process of evolution, it becomes clear that the Book of Genesis actually does discuss evolution. The term, evolution (when referring to biological descent with modification), was used by Herbert Spencer in the late 1800's, so it should not be expected to be in the Bible. Since the evolutionary process is a "natural process that created the diversity of life", then we should be looking in the Bible for a statement similar to this.

When God created the sea creatures, he did not just say, "Let there be sea creatures and birds", he gave this task to the sea:

-"And God said, *Let the waters bring forth abundantly* the moving creature that hath life, and *fowl* that may fly above the earth in the open firmament of heaven." (Genesis 1:20 KJV)

Later, when God created the plants and the land animals, he used the same process, but with the earth forming the creatures instead of the sea:

-"And God said, *Let the earth bring forth* the living creature after his kind, cattle, and creeping thing, and beast of the earth after his kind: and it was so." (Genesis 1:24 KJV)

When taken too literally, Genesis 2:19 seems to contradict both Genesis 1:20 and 1:24 by stating that fowl came from the "ground" not from the "sea" and stating that the beasts of the field also came from the "ground" and not the "earth".

-"And out of the *ground* the LORD God formed every beast of the field, and every fowl of the air..." (Genesis 2:19)

If both *sea* and *earth* are synonymous with *ground* then the contradiction goes away. Taking Genesis 2:19 into consideration, the only logical interpretation is that God used the nature (land and sea) to form the diversity of life. In other words, a natural process formed the diversity of life, and this conforms to the process of evolution. To consider that God then interfered with his natural process by using unnatural miracles to create life would be to accept that God is not true to his Word. He gave the entire job to the sea and the earth. Additionally, this seems to question God's omnipotence (and omniscience) if the natural laws he put into place could not do the job.

Did this same natural process also form man, or was he separate and unique? Was man made fully formed? Consider the following verse:

-"then the LORD God formed man of dust from the *ground,* and breathed into his nostrils the breath of life; and man became a living being." (Genesis 2:7)

Genesis 2:19 states that the other animals were formed from "out of the ground", just as Genesis 2:7 proclaims. It suggests that man is a product of the same natural process as the rest of life. This interpretation is not only consistent with the process of evolution; it is also consistent with the facts.

# Chapter 8 – The Heart has Reasons that Reason Ignores

*The heart has reasons that reason ignores.*
- Blaise Pascal (1623-1662)

A murder case took place in the state of Virginia in 1982 involving suspect, Roger Keith Coleman. He was charged with raping and murdering his sister-in-law, Wanda McCoy, in her home, or just outside, on March 10, 1981. Coleman pleaded not guilty. The jury was directed to stick to the facts of the case, listen to the arguments on both sides, and then make a conclusion based upon the facts. Less fact-based but still mandatory were eyewitness testimonies they had to make decisions upon. The jurors came up with a verdict of guilty and convicted Coleman of rape and murder.

Ten years later in 1992 the state of Virginia executed Roger Keith Coleman for this murder, yet he maintained his innocence to the very end. Minister James McCloskey, executive director of Centurion Ministries believed Coleman's story, and had been fighting to prove his innocence since 1988. McCloskey finally convinced the State of Virginia to undergo a DNA testing on sperm found inside the victim. In January 2006, the results came back and they were positive for having come from Roger Keith Coleman. The test results confirmed Coleman's guilt. Upon receiving this information, McCloskey stated,

"I had always *believed* in Roger's complete innocence. In my view, he had no motive, means, or opportunity to do this crime. I now *know* that I was wrong."

When listening to McCloskey speak prior to the DNA test, it was obvious he had complete confidence in Coleman's innocence. What convinced the jury of his guilt was that Coleman actually did have motive, means, and opportunity. Among other evidence, he had a prior conviction for rape, he was near McCoy's house the night of the murder, and he had access to it. McCloskey even knew something the jury did not know; he failed a polygraph test. His intuition, along with a few selected facts, made him believe Coleman was an honest man doomed by a series of unfortunate coincidences. In this case, his reason to ignore reason failed him.

This leads us to the most harmful roadblock in the search for truth; wishful thinking. At some point, human beings make the decision to either believe or not believe, and understanding what pulls our cognitive decision-making strings has a direct bearing upon reaching the truth. We need to know why the heart has reasons to ignore reason; one of the most effective tools in truth searching.

The words *truth* and *true* have a number of connotations. For the purpose of clarity, we are going to consider the definition of truth as "what is correct". According Dr. Ronald Giere, professor emeritus of philosophy at University of Minnesota, truth is objective reality, which means any event or object independent of the conscious awareness of it. For example, if the butler committed the murder, then the butler being the murderer is the truth, regardless if anyone believes that he is or not. We are going to consider the definition of true to be "when someone accepts something as the truth". It may not necessarily be the truth, but it has been embraced as the truth. It is a subjective reality, or reality in the mind of the believer. "I believe it is true that the butler is the murderer." In short, truth is an external reality, while true is an internal acceptance of reality.

This leads to the evaluation of two additional words, *believing* and *knowing.* These also have multiple connotations, but for the same reason of clarity, we will focus upon only two. Differentiating these two words may sound like semantics, but it is not. Believing something and knowing something are two different ways that people accept information as being true. They are cognitive, or mental, processes of decision-making. Decision-making encompasses many areas, but we are going to focus strictly upon how human beings accept or deny the validity of information, since this has a direct bearing upon the evolution/creation controversy.

Thanks to both nature and nurture, we gregarious human beings form a system of values and principles, which give us the social skills to successfully interact with other human beings. Values are ideas that are important to us or ideas that we stand for and principles are standards we live by based upon those values. A value system is the summation of our ethical values, such as assessing right from wrong, good from bad, and our ideological values, such as assessing societal norms, religion, and politics. Believing can be defined as accepting as true through the use of our value system. For example, one may believe it is wrong to kill another human being, because killing violates a number of ethical values, such as the right to life and the fair treatment of all.

Knowing can be defined as accepting as true through the use of our intellect. Cognition is the logical process of learning, reasoning, and knowing. Knowing is a variant word of knowledge. Knowing is not subject to our value system like believing is; it is based upon information and logical connections between information. For example, McCloskey finally knew Coleman was guilty of raping and murdering his sister-in-law, because the DNA evidence confirmed this conclusion.

Knowing and believing defined in these two ways is supported by the following two phrases, "Why do you believe..." and "How do you know...?" *Why* suggests a value-based internal source and *how* suggests a fact-based external source. Believing seeks something internally subjective and knowing seeks something externally objective. Another way of simplifying the difference between believing and knowing is with the following phrase, "Believing comes from your heart and knowing comes from your head." For years, many have known that people make decisions from both their heart and their head. Recall the quote from Pascal, which was stated nearly four hundred years ago: "The heart has reasons that reason ignores." Notice that Pascal, a 17th century French mathematician, physicist, and religious philosopher, realized the human mind makes decisions in two different ways, from the heart and from reason, or the head.

## The Amazing Human Brain

In 1973, Dr. Robert Axelrod published his research on schema theory. He stated that the human mind organizes decision-making processes into mental constructs, or pathways, called *schema*. He concluded that these mental pathways are formed as we grow and experience life. It is a hard wiring of the mind for humans to make decisions based upon both our value system and our intellect. The two schemas specific to the decision-making act of accepting or denying the truth are the *affective pathway* and the *cognitive pathway*. The affective pathway encompasses our emotions, such as feelings, appreciation, enthusiasms, motivations, values, and attitudes. Notice how the word "affectionate" is a variant word of affective. The cognitive pathway encompasses the intellect. The intellect involves recall and recognition, comprehension, application, analysis, synthesis, and evaluation. It is the core of critical thinking.

Is there any corroborative physical evidence supporting the schema theory where the human mind actually makes decisions both emotionally and intellectually? Cognitive neuroscientists using functional magnetic resonance imaging (fMRI) have discovered that the human mind does indeed make decisions in these two ways. Tested subjects were given different decision-making scenarios while being connected to the fMRI instrument. The fMRI records the blood flow pattern in the brain, which shows the functioning parts of the brain during a decision-making process. Dr. Benedetto de Martino of the University College Institute of Neurology in London, England, along with his team used fMRI and demonstrated that purely emotional decision-making follows the *limbic system*, or our emotional center, of the brain. It is the part of the brain that controls emotion, motivation, and emotional associations with memory. Intellectual reasoning in decision-making was observed to activate the *cerebral cortex*, specifically the prefrontal cortex region of the frontal lobes, our intellectual center.

Before discussing why human beings make decisions both emotionally and intellectually, we need to talk about the structure of our brain. Briefly, the human brain can be separated into three distinct parts, or tiers, from the most basic tier to the most advanced tier. The first tier is the *brain stem*, which is the innermost section of the brain. It sits directly on top of the spine, and operates the most basic functions of our dynamic body. All back-boned animals in the animal kingdom, which includes fish, amphibians, reptiles, birds, and mammals, share this feature. It is sometimes called the reptilian brain. The second tier is the emotional limbic system, which covers and surrounds the brain stem. Not all back-boned animals have a limbic system, such as the more primitive fish and amphibians, and some have very small ones, such as reptiles. Mammals and birds, on the other hand, have a larger and well organized limbic system. This part of the brain is sometimes called the mammalian brain. It allows for more complex social organization with stronger emotional bonds than fish, amphibians, and reptiles. For example, most reptiles merely lay their eggs and then leave with no emotional attachments to their offspring, while birds and mammals take it a step further and care for their young even after hatching or birth.

The last tier of the brain is our intellectual cerebral cortex. It surrounds both the reptilian and mammalian parts of the brain. The cerebral cortex controls higher order thinking skills. Less intelligent mammals have a small cerebral cortex, while progressively more intelligent mammals have a correspondingly larger cerebral cortex. According to Dr. Simón, professor of neuroscience at the University of Valencia in Spain, cats have a cerebral cortex that makes up approximately 3% of their brain, the chimpanzee's cerebral cortex makes up approximately 17%, while the human being's cerebral cortex makes up approximately 33% of their brain. It should not be a surprise that intellectual decision-making with humans occurs at a higher frequency and with greater complexity than all other species.

This particular three-tiered brain structure, the inner reptilian, the middle mammalian, and the outer human, also conforms to common ancestry. Our most ancient and primitive back-boned ancestors possessed only the inner brain stem. Millions of years later, our distant ancestors possessed both the inner brain stem and a progressively larger limbic system in order to successfully interact in a complex and more advantageous social structure. The limbic system would naturally be positioned over the brain stem, since it evolved after the brain stem. Lastly, our more recent primate ancestors progressively developed a larger and more complex cerebral cortex over the limbic system, allowing more intelligent and advantageous decision-making. This would also suggest that our emotional decision-making pathway was in place well before our intellectual decision-making pathway, and that the intellectual pathway was designed to augment, not replace, the emotional pathway.

If it is correct that our three-tiered brain structure was formed through the evolutionary process, then we should see progressively larger braincases in the fossils of our human ancestors. This is exactly what we see. Brain casts of the primitive australopithecines were similar in size to Chimpanzees. The next oldest fossil skulls are of *Homo habilis* and they have slightly larger brain casts, while the even younger fossil skulls of *Homo erectus* have progressively larger brain casts. Finally, early *Homo sapien* fossil brain casts are even larger than Homo erectus.

## The Emotional Method of Making Decisions

Does emotional and intellectual decision-making operate independently, or do they interact with each other? Research by Dr.

Antonio Damasio at UCLA has confirmed that decision-making is an unbreakable integration between both the emotional pathway and the intellectual pathway. According to fMRI data, they are constantly interacting with each other. Dr. Damasio explains that as a person creates a thought, the mind automatically attaches an emotion from the limbic system to that thought. This thought/emotion packet is called a *somatic marker*, which allows a person to recognize the implications of an experience. This means that even the most intellectual decisions have an emotional component, such as if I discover the answer to a mathematical problem, I experience an emotional feeling of satisfaction.

Possessing two mental pathways at our disposal (an emotional pathway and an intellectual pathway) has also created two entirely different methods of decision-making. The first can be called the *emotional method of decision-making*. Recall that as a thought comes to mind (new or preexisting), a somatic marker is formed, i.e., an emotion from the limbic system becomes attached to the thought as one recognizes its implications. In the case of a claim or argument, a positive emotion is attached to the thought if one is in agreement or a negative emotion is attached if one is in disagreement. An initial decision to accept (or not to accept) is made through the emotional pathway. Only after this is the intellectual pathway integrated in an attempt to now logically justify the particular emotional experience.

Ideally, if the facts refute the belief, one will change their opinion and correct the belief just as McCloskey did. In emotional decision-making, confidence that a claim or argument is true comes when an opinion is supported by strong evidence and good logic. Since the emotional center of our brain is the more basal and primitive than the intellectual center, the human mind is hard-wired to use the emotional method of decision-making. This method of decision-making is custom made for issues of the heart, such as politics. Politics is all about values, principles, and opinions, such as opinions on funding special projects, effects of the economy on our lives, accepting stem cell research or not, and believing in abortion or pro-life. Making political decisions based upon ones principles is called *ideology*.

An example of the effective use of emotional decision-making in everyday life is an experience my wife and I recently had. We were witness to two people in a meeting having a heated argument over a job related issue. To me, the dispute did not warrant such a loud and long confrontation, so it seemed to me that the real problem was a personality conflict between the two. I felt that they just did not like each other. My wife then whispered to me, "I bet they are having an affair." Known to both of us was that the man was single and the woman was married. My wife then said, "I know how women react, and she is acting like a scorned lover." My wife believed the two were having an affair, because of a gut feeling, *i.e.,* her intuition. Justification came from seeing a familiar pattern of female behavior. Before my wife expressed her opinion to me, I was oblivious to this possibility. I am the first to admit that my intuition is relatively weak in the area of human relationships. Even after listening to my wife's claim, I was skeptical. Two months later, it was revealed that the two were indeed having an affair. My wife's intuition was correct. The argument we witnessed was all the evidence she needed to logically justify her belief. In this case, the emotional method of decision-making worked well.

### The Intellectual Method of Making Decisions

The second method of decision-making can be called the *intellectual method of decision-making*. It emphasizes not the emotional pathway, but the intellectual pathway. Intellectual decision-making attempts to ignore the emotion that attaches to a thought (the somatic marker) in order to concentrate strictly upon higher order thinking skills. We value this process of decision-making, because we have since realized the effectiveness of logical thinking. Also, we have realized that any emotional investment just might create a bias in our conclusions. This decision-making process begins by objectively evaluating the facts and then ends by making a conclusion based upon these facts. Notice how we do not begin with a conclusion, or opinion, as in the case with emotional decision-making, but we end with one. The idea is to avoid jumping to any conclusions before evaluating the facts.

This method is not a natural method of thinking for human beings, since our minds are designed to integrate our intellect with our emotions. If human beings could bypass the emotional aspect, then personal bias would be a non-issue. Every decision would be purely objective. One area of human endeavor that gets closest to a totally objective method of decision-making is modern science. Because scientists are human beings and the scientific community recognizes our inherent emotional biases, part of graduate education is to develop objectivity through controlled research. Even with emotion at its core, the mind can still be conditioned to maintain or improve objectivity prior to making a decision. It must be a conscious act of ignoring preconceived ideas and beliefs, which will ideally become a habit in thinking. The beauty of this method is that it is a way for humans to avoid emotional bias, which has always been a source for human error. The goal is to have a scientific conclusion not influenced by conjecture or wishful thinking. This is the point Charles Darwin was making when he stated:

"A scientific man ought to have no wishes, no affections, - a mere heart of stone."

In practice, personal bias does creep into the minds of scientists. It is unavoidable, so a process of peer review is incorporated into the scientific process for all published research. Step three is to keep the research on the chopping blocks for future experts to continuously evaluate it in light of new evidence. This is an excellent place to clarify the difference between scientists and science. Scientists are human beings trained to ignore emotional decision-making, but the human mind guarantees an element of emotion involved. The scientific process, on the other hand, is not an entity with an emotional brain. It is a procedural tool for the purpose of discovering the realities of nature. Through years of improvements, it has been fine-tuned to best eliminate conjecture and personal bias. The scientific process takes into account the fallibility of human beings, and there are steps in place in order to minimize human error.

The intellectual decision-making process can also be seen used in the judicial system. To ensure that only the guilty are convicted, an adversarial system of justice is employed. Personal bias can cloud judgment, and the judicial system recognizes this human natural tendency. Before the case begins, the jury is directed to put aside any preconceived notions, and make a decision based solely upon the facts of the case. Before the jury renders a decision on the case, both sides have been given the opportunity to present their best possible argument. In effect, the jurors are told to use the empirical version of the intellectual method of decision-making. Ideally, the jurors will become conditioned into maintaining objectivity. Although not perfect, the adversarial system of justice has a record of success. For the most part, the guilty are convicted while the innocent are not. If all of the evidence is taken into account before making a conclusion, then a picture of truth just might reveal itself.

Although science desires to eliminate emotion entirely, the judicial system still has a need for it. For example, a juror must use their *intuition* in order to evaluate the trustworthiness and credibility of a witness. The dictionary definition of intuition is "accepting as true without recourse to facts and reason", which is what they are asked to do. The definition needs to be clarified, though. Intuition does use facts, but instead of empirical evidence as the definition is referring to, intuition uses experience-based evidence, as in the case of my wife recognizing the reactions of a scorned woman. To evaluate eyewitness testimony with the least amount of bias entering into the picture, the jury is given a *falsus in uno* criminal instruction as a guide for listening to eyewitness testimony. It says that if any part of a witness's testimony is contradictory in any way, then jurors have the right to disregard none, some, or all of their testimony. It comes from the complete Latin phrase, *falsus in uno, falsus in omnibus*, which means "untrue in one thing, untrue in everything". The courts recognize that human error, bias, and deception are an inevitable part of testimonial evidence. The fault lies not in the intellectual pathway, but in the emotional pathway.

**An Example of Integration**

Taking Dr. Damasio's discoveries into consideration, human beings often take advantage of both decision-making processes in order to effectively discover the truth. Take for example a murder case. After the murder, a crime scene investigation ensues. The investigation begins with crime scene recognition, followed by documentation, finding the evidence, collecting the evidence, and then analyzing the evidence. The investigators are using the intellectual method of decision-making in order to make sense of the case. Detectives assigned to the case will also use the intellectual method of decision-making as they create a list of suspects. When the suspects are investigated and evaluated and the list narrows to one probable suspect, decision-making may begin to shift. As a detective finally becomes convinced of the guilt of one particular suspect, his or her attention, time, and energy is now focused upon that suspect. This new motivation and focus is an affective response, meaning it is a product of the emotional method of decision-making. The detective is now attempting to justify his or her belief with the discovery of new evidence. In one respect, the emotional method of decision-making has an advantage over the intellectual method, because of the increased level of persistence and drive associated with it. Tenacity is an excellent quality for a detective to effectively catch a murderer, *as long as it is focused upon the right person.*

**Bypassing the Intellect – Fight or Flight**

At times, the intellect is bypassed entirely during the decision-making process. On the surface, bypassing the intellect may seem like a bad decision, but not in all cases. It may occur if an unusually intense emotion is attached to a thought, such as fear. This type of somatic marker immediately sparks adrenaline flow, which increases the heart rate in preparation for the body to go into action. Decision-making in this case bypasses the cerebral cortex and goes straight to the brain stem and limbic system. The body is in fight-or-flight mode. According to Dr. Simón, bypassing the cerebral cortex is the shortest and fastest method of decision-making. The advantage to this method is speed. It allows for quick action if you find yourself in the way of a fast-moving truck. A personal example of this method is when I recently found myself potentially late for work one morning. Each evening I set my alarm at 5:45 AM, which allows me enough time to calmly wake up, shower & shave, and then make it safely to work with time to spare. On this particular day, my daughter came into my bedroom, woke me up and said, "Dad, aren't you suppose to be up?" I looked up at the clock and it showed 7:00 AM. Once I comprehended the situation and recognized the implications of waking up so late, a huge fear emotion attached itself to this thought. This flood of emotion caused me to swear, leap out of bed, abbreviate my morning tasks, and drive aggressively to work. I did make it to work on time, but in the process I strained my back as I jumped out of bed, accidentally woke the baby up, yelled at the dog, left my cell phone at home, and wore different colored socks to work.

Dr. Simón explains that the use of this emotion-only method in decision-making is the most primitive method. As stated earlier, our brains are the result of a naturalistic process of biological evolution and common ancestry. This explains why the more basic emotional pathway continues to be the default pathway during times of high stress. Taken further, since the brain was initially designed emotionally and the intellectual component was a later add-on for assistance, it explains why tend to emotionally accept a claim, or believe, and only then intellectually justify the belief. It also explains why human beings need to be conditioned in order to correctly use the intellectual method of decision-making as in the case of a juror.

## Wishful Thinking

*Wishful thinking* is defined as, "The formation of beliefs and making decisions according to what might be pleasing to imagine instead of by appealing to evidence or rationality". This means that wishful thinking is an aspect of the emotional method of decision-making, since the act of pleasing is an emotion. If we take into account Dr. Simón's discovery that the emotional pathway is the fastest and more primitive, thus, default pathway and the intellectual pathway was a later enhancement, by extension human beings have a natural tendency towards wishful thinking rather than towards an objective search for truth. McCloskey so much wanted Roger Keith Coleman to be innocent; it took overwhelming evidence to the contrary to finally accept his guilt.

The emotional struggle between wishful thinking and objectivity can be seen in what psychologists call *accommodation vs. assimilation.* According to Jean Piaget (1896-1980), a Swiss developmental psychologist, as human beings internalize new information (or experiences), they either assimilate, or incorporate this information into their unaltered beliefs, or they accommodate, or alter their beliefs in order to fit the new information. When McCloskey heard that Roger Keith Coleman failed the polygraph test, this did not alter his belief that Coleman was innocent of the rape and murder. He assimilated the new information into his beliefs by explaining away the trustworthiness of polygraph tests. Thanks to the structure of our brain, it is much easier to assimilate this rather than to accommodate it and admit ones beliefs are wrong.

An example of accommodation can be seen when UC Davis psychology professor Dr. Phil Shaver interviewed the Dalia Lama and asked him what he would do "if he found out some belief that he holds as part of his tradition were shown to be wrong." The Dalai Lama replied that "he would change his belief and tell his followers to do the same." If the Dalia Lama holds true to this comment, then this would be a case of appealing to evidence or rationality, as opposed to wishful thinking.

According to Dr. Leon Festinger (1919-1989), an American social psychologist, when one recognizes a disparity between what they believe and what they know, an internal psychological tension occurs. This state of internal conflict is called *cognitive dissonance*. It is defined as,

"A psychological phenomenon which refers to the discomfort felt at a discrepancy between what you already *know* or *believe*, and new information or interpretation."

According to Festinger, human beings have an irresistible drive to alleviate this feeling. It can be likened to wanting to take out an irritating pebble from ones shoe. Festinger further explained that we alleviate this stress in one of three ways. First, one can accommodate to the new information by amending ones belief system, as in the case with the Dalia Lama. As stated earlier, the human mind does not initially prefer this, but the intellect may eventually win out. Second, one can completely ignore the issue. If the issue is of little value, then it is much easier for the mind to ignore the new information. Third, one can "add more consonant beliefs than dissonant beliefs" in an attempt to satisfactorily assimilate the new information. This third way is a version of confirmation bias where one is merely convincing themselves of the truth by emphasizing supporting evidence and de-emphasizing contradictory evidence. If this is the case, the goal of objectively searching for truth is now playing second fiddle to wishful thinking. I call this *searching for truth with a broken flashlight*. Just as a broken flashlight cannot illuminate, or reveal from darkness, succumbing to wishful thinking cannot guarantee one is on the path to truth. It is still an act of searching for truth, because the person honestly believes they are correct, but the goal is something other than reaching the truth.

# Chapter 9 – Of Mongrels and Milkmen

*Truth, like milk, arrives in the dark*
*But even so, wise dogs don't bark.*
*Only mongrels make it hard*
*For the milkman to come up the yard.*
-Christopher Morley, *Dogs Don't Bark at the Milkman*

In the spring of 1997, members of a cult called Heaven's Gate led by Marshall Applewhite committed mass suicide by drinking a lethal mixture of Phenobarbital and vodka. The members believed that Applewhite was Jesus reincarnated. There was no evidence for this, but they believed it without any doubt. This belief was so strong that they followed Applewhite into death. Applewhite explained to his cult members that "inner beings" in a spacecraft traveling alongside comet Hale-Bopp are coming for them. He told them they must commit suicide so that their inner beings will be transported onto the spaceship. The spaceship will then take them to another planet where their cult co-founder, Bonnie Nettles (who had recently died of cancer), is waiting for them.

Interestingly, members of Heaven's Gate bought an expensive telescope just prior to Earth's encounter with comet Hale-Bopp, but they returned it soon after. The storeowner asked why they were returning the telescope. They claimed that it was defective because they could not see the spacecraft! Their belief was so strong that the possibility of there not being a spacecraft next to Comet Hale-Bopp was completely out of the question. Contradictory physical evidence did little to weaken their belief that a spacecraft was on its way. Applewhite and his followers believed in a form of Gnosticism where everything in the physical world is evil, including physical evidence. It was completely logical in their minds that contradictory evidence from the physical world was flawed, but notice the circular mental trap they had put themselves into. Once they totally believed in Marshall Applewhite's worldview, there was literally nothing on this physical Earth that could convince them otherwise. Since Applewhite was Jesus Christ in their minds, not even the Bible could change their minds. They became a prisoner of assimilation. The possibility of accommodating their beliefs to new and contradictory evidence was no longer an option, especially when waiving in these beliefs was most likely considered a weakness in faith. The assimilation circular trap was set and Applywhite's followers were effectively brainwashed.

**Milkmen or Mongrels?**

Less dramatic than voluntarily committing suicide but of critical importance in the evolution/creation controversy are how certain dogmatic anti-evolution creationists have gotten caught in their own assimilation circular trap. As with most devout Christians, they have accepted by faith that their Christian beliefs are the absolute truth. Additionally though, they believe the Holy Spirit has inspired their particular interpretation of the Bible, thus, is also an absolute truth. Because of this, any physical evidence or claim to the contrary must be wrong, since it conflicts with these absolute truths. Lastly, wavering on these beliefs is due entirely to ones weakness in faith. The only possible option when confronted with new and contradictory information is to assimilate it into their set beliefs, not unlike the case of the members of Heaven's Gate.

A big difference between Applewhite and dogmatic anti-evolution creationists is that the latter claim all physical evidence supports their conclusions, which means scientists are just plain wrong. So, the question then becomes as they evangelize to the public, are they honestly presenting the truth or are they impeding the truth by attempting to convince you of their personal beliefs? In the words of Christopher Morley, are they milkmen or are they mongrels?

## Reverend Carl Baugh and Kent Hovind

Consider a few cases involving young earth creationist Reverend Carl Baugh. Ever since the early twentieth century, young earth creationists have used the Paluxy River man tracks near Glenn Rose, Texas, as clear proof humans and dinosaurs coexisted. Alongside dinosaur tracks molded into limestone rocks at the base of the Paluxy River are what seem to be giant human footprints. If correct, this would support the creationist's flood geology claim that all of the layer sedimentary rocks are remnant global flood deposits from the time of Noah. It would also completely refute the theory of evolution, and in so doing, question the validity of the entire scientific process.

Stanley Taylor's 1972 film, *Footprints in Stone,* and John Morris' book, *Tracking Those Incredible Dinosaurs and the People Who Knew Them* (1982), highlighted this evidence. Carl Baugh, a Baptist minister, has been a big proponent of the man tracks. He has headed nonscientific research at the Paluxy River, and operates a small museum out of Glen Rose, Texas. He was also used as an expert on the 1996 NBC pseudoscience program, *The Mysterious Origins of Man.* Many like-minded Christians all over the world embraced this as physical proof of their belief, even though paleontologists outright dismissed the claim because it conflicted with scientific evidence. To Christians, scientists were either so stupid as to not recognize the facts or so blinded by Satan that they were helpless to see the truth.

Recently, the major young earth creationist organizations, such as the Institute for Creation Research (ICR) and Answers in Genesis (AIG), have finally accepted the "man tracks" claim to be invalid. The so-called human footprints are, in fact, dinosaur footprints. An interesting weathering phenomenon occurred to the tracks after decades of being exposed to the air. The three-tocd dinosaur imprints that were at first hidden from view on the footprints gradually changed color and became visible. As this weathering process began to expose the true nature of the footprints, creationist defenders of the man

163 ‖

tracks initially attempted to assimilate the new information into their threatened dinosaur footprint belief, but most young earth creationists have since reluctantly admitted that the tracks were from dinosaurs. Even with this new evidence Carl Baugh, and young earth creationist Kent Hovind, still claim the footprints are from giant humans. This is a classic case of assimilation without the possibility of accommodation. Further, they continue to promote this to a believing community unaware that the leading anti-evolution creationists now reject it. Are they milkmen or mongrels?

Incidentally, Reverend Baugh also has a TV show called *Creation in the 21st Century* on the *Trinity Broadcast Network*. At the beginning of the show, he claims that they,

> "...come to a scientific and logical conclusion that a creator designed the universe, based on the evidence."

The show then attempts to convince the audience of the young earth creationist claim that the Earth is only 6,000 years old. For me as a science educator and as a Christian, I have a major issue with this statement. I do not question the claim that a creator designed the universe, but I do question Reverend Baugh's claim that he can come to a valid scientific conclusion. As I stated earlier, the purpose of science is to discover the mysteries of nature, not super-nature. Science requires a cause and effect relationship in order to eliminate the wrong answers and end up with the right one. Accepting supernatural explanations in science renders this process useless. If a rock is magically created, then it is physically impossible for science to test this event, since there is no cause (formation of the rock) of the effect (the rock).

Also, does Reverend Baugh really use a scientific approach on his TV show? Because the scientific process is strictly a cognitive method of decision-making, it ignores the affective method. The problem for Reverend Baugh is that he begins his truth searching with a belief just as he does in his sermons, i.e., the emotional method of decision-making. Even his beginning statement insinuates this process, "…that a creator designed the universe". This is precisely why the scientific community rejects his research. It merely violates the rules of the game.

Reverend Baugh could still be effectively using the emotional method of decision-making in the search for truth, or is he caught in the assimilation circular trap as in the case of the Paluxy River man tracks? The emotional method may not be scientific, but at least the goal is discovering the truth. If there were any examples of Baugh knowingly accepting questionable evidence to support his belief, then this would indicate altering information in order to fit set beliefs, i.e., assimilation. A quick look at young earth creationist websites reveals that many fellow young earth creationists seriously question Carl Baugh's methods (AIG, ICR, etc.). Why do many fellow young earth creationists reject Baugh's claims? The answer is that Baugh is indeed passing off a number of questionable pieces of evidence for credible evidence. He claims (as does young earth creationist Kent Hovind) that there are thousands of ancient Ica stones discovered in Peru that picture man and dinosaurs together. Dr. Javier Cabrera of Peru has collected these engraved stones from a farmer. The farmer claimed to find the stones in a cave. Recently, this farmer was arrested for selling the stones to tourists, and he told police that there was no cave and he was actually making the stone engravings himself. Incidentally, even if the engravings were real, they depict creatures with five toes. There were no dinosaurs with five toes.

Another example of Baugh accepting questionable evidence, yet passing it off to the *Creation in the 21st Century* audience for credible evidence, is the London Artifact. The London Artifact is an old looking hammer supposedly found embedded in ancient rock, which would then be proof that the rock layers are remnant global flood sediment and are merely thousands of years old as opposed to millions of years old. He claims that the London Artifact is a hammer used during the time of Noah. Recently, it has been discovered what the London Artifact actually is. About a dozen of these hammers have since been found at Scott's Bluff, Nebraska, and they were used to fix wagon wheels during the horse drawn wagon days of the old American West. The claim that the London Artifact was discovered embedded in rock should now be questioned, especially since the collector of the evidence has a hidden personal agenda other than truth.

**Steve Austin and the Institute for Creation Research**

This case involves one of the top young earth creationist organizations, the Institute for Creation Research (ICR). In January 1998, a group of scientists and skeptics visited the Museum of Creation Earth History operated by the ICR in California. Steve Austin, the resident geologist for the ICR, was selected to give a lecture to this group, and began the lecture by showing a video of the 1980 Mount St. Helens eruption. He then told the group that he had once been an evolutionist, but his observations of these deposits converted him to a young earth creationist. This meant his conversion to young earth creationism would have been in 1980.

In the 1970s, there was a young earth creationist writer who published for the ICR under the pseudonym, Stewart Nevins. One of the members of this group asked Austin if he knew this Stewart Nevins. Austin then admitted that he was Nevins. This makes his Mount St. Helens testimony an outright lie, since Austin clearly believed in a young earth prior to the Mount St. Helens eruption. Why did he do this? He is using a convincing persuasion tactic. If an expert in science gets converted to believing in young earth creationism, then this would lend credibility to young earth arguments in the eyes of the general public. It would show that a fellow scientist was convinced based upon objective facts and upon a religious belief. Instead, the fact that he admitted deception clearly indicates Austin has been caught in an assimilation circular trap ever since the 1970's.

By the way, if someone is honestly searching for truth, then how can the ICR organization be considered a credible source? The ICR was fully aware of the deception, since they published Stewart Nevins' articles in the 1970's.

## The Discovery Institute and Intelligent Design

A new spin on creationism began in the 1990's; called Intelligent Design (ID). The Discovery Institute is the Intelligent Design organization that began this movement. The Discovery Institute was not its first name, though. They use to call themselves The Center for the Renewal of Science and Culture. Publicly, ID proponents claim they are merely presenting a more complete science involving a creator. "We are merely promoting that there was a creator involved in the creation of the life and the universe." They claim that they are not trying to eliminate evolution from the science classrooms, but they merely want to teach the controversy in objective scientific form. They want the American student exposed to both sides of the issue, the evidence for evolution and the evidence against evolution. At the surface, this seems like a very honest goal, but if we dig further we will find that they are not being honest. Privately, they have a loftier goal. Their plan is to cause a major cultural change away from the anti-God materialism and toward a Christian-based system. They have targeted evolutionary theory, since they view this as the cornerstone of the anti-God philosophy. In 1999, when they were still called The Center for the Renewal of Science and Culture, they accidentally posted their organizational agenda onto their website. They soon realized posting it was a mistake, because it revealed their biased hidden agenda, so they immediately took it off their website. Their organizational agenda is an internal planning document called the *Wedge Strategy,* which explains to members the organization's short-term, mid-term, and long-term goals. The long-term agenda is to Christianize American culture by using the "thin edge of the wedge" to tear down "scientific materialism" and replace it with supernaturalism. Their short-term and mid-term goals are in place to best achieve their long-term goal. This report can be found at *www.anti-evolution.org/features/wedge. html*.

The ID movement was dealt a major blow in September of 2005 when U.S. District Judge John E. Jones ruled in the case of *Kitzmiller v. Dover Area School District* that allowing intelligent design into the public science classroom violates the constitutional separation of church and state. Judge Jones said, "We find that the secular purposes claimed by the board amount to a pretext for the board's real purpose, which was to promote religion in the public school classroom." He also said that intelligent design advocates "have bona fide and deeply held beliefs which drive their scholarly endeavors." In other words, research by intelligent design proponents is not entirely objective.

In each one of the above cases anti-evolution creationists are blatantly deceiving the public in order to push their hidden agenda, while sacrificing an objective search for truth. Would they be considered milkmen or mongrels?

# Chapter 10 – Seek Resonance and Avoid Dissonance

*Fraud and falsehood only dread examination. Truth invites it.* –
Thomas Cooper (1759-1839)

In the spring of 2003, the United States and coalition forces were dominating the Iraqi forces and finally entering the city of Baghdad. Mohammed Saeed Al-Sahaf, the Minister of Information for Saddam Hussein, became known as "Baghdad Bob – the Minister of Disinformation", because of the daily disinformation he was spreading on TV for those last few weeks of the military conflict. His comments were in stark contrast to the claims the U.S. military, along with the western press, was giving about the progress of the battles.

The following are some of his comments: "No, there are no Americans at the airport (and there were)", "Our estimates are that none of them will come out alive unless they surrender to us quickly", "We have them surrounded in their tanks", "These are not Iraqi POWs. They are not Iraqi soldiers at all. Where did they bring them from?", "…over the past few days, we managed to shoot down 196 missiles…", "Iraq will not be defeated. Iraq has now already achieved victory apart from a few technicalities", and as the American forces were entering Baghdad, Al-Sahaf stated, "They are not even within 100 miles of Baghdad…this is an illusion…they are trying to sell an illusion."

For the American public, it was quite obvious that Al-Sahaf was lying, since a relatively trustworthy press was "embedded" into the U.S. military units. Aside from some minor political spins, the press is generally seen as reliable to Americans. The press' credibility would have been reduced to nothing if it were later revealed they were lying.

The opposite belief was happening in the Muslim world. Many had succumbed to their wishful thinking, and believed Al-Sahaf's version of events. An American news agency began interviewing Muslim citizens in a number of Middle East countries known to have a negative stereotype of the U.S., and it was apparent that a very large percentage of them believed Al-Sahaf's version of events. I recall thinking that when the dust settles these people will experience a big shock, and that is exactly what happened. Follow up interviews of these Muslim citizens showed that they were stunned by Al-Sahaf's deception. They believed so strongly the United States was lying, probably because of their anti-American conditioning, that they denied the evidence until it became irrefutable. In other words, they had been assimilating what they believed was the usual United States deceptive propaganda to such an extent that when reality hit their worldview no longer made sense. Accommodating to the fact that the United States and the western press were truthful in this case became a tough pill to swallow.

The "Baghdad Bob" case is not an example of an error in a people's faith, but it is an example of how wishful thinking can be so strong that belief can hijack the decision-making process. Most of us in the U.S. were wise to Al-Sahaf's deceptions, but those of us who consider our faith an important part of our life can get bamboozled just as easily. A well-known televangelist and faith healer, Peter Popoff, gained national recognition in the 1980's for his ability to heal people with the power of God. Popoff would hold faith-healings, and have the audience members fill out prayer cards. He would then miraculously speak out specific illnesses and names of believers in the audience, and then put his hand upon them and healed them of their ailments. Millions of honest Christians believed in his miracles, so much so that he earned millions of dollars and became a national figure.

In 1987, skeptic and magician James Randi had a private investigator secretly record faith-healing sessions with a scanner and tape recorder. The scanner picked up Popoff's wife, Elizabeth, saying,

"Petey, can you hear me?" She was secretly reading the prayer cards to Popoff through a radio into his hidden earphone. On the Tonight Show with Johnny Carson, Randi showed a clip of Popoff deceptively yelling to the audience, "Harold". Popoff's wife then said in the earphone, "Cataracts". Popoff followed with, "God is going to burn those cataracts right off your eyes!" Randi stated to Carson, "Popoff says God tells him these things. Maybe he does. But I didn't realize God used a frequency of 39.17 megahertz and had a voice exactly like Elizabeth Popoff's."

Both, Al-Sahaf and Popoff, purposely deceived their audiences. They had hidden agendas that had nothing to do with truth. The above quote by Thomas Cooper, an American educationalist and political philosopher, offers us help in discovering the truth. The solution is honest examination. Since truth invites examination, then examination is the path to truth.

### Inviting Examination

Resonance means a fit, or match, between two things has been made. For example, when DNA evidence confirms that a convicted killer committed the crime, the DNA evidence resonates with a jury's previous decision to convict. *Cognitive resonance* is when a belief fits well with a logical conclusion. It is an emotional state of satisfaction. Professors Lee, Chun, and Kim express it this way:

"Cognitive resonance is believed to be generated in a decision maker's psychology and mental realm when emotional schema fits well with rational schema."

Pertinent to issues involving faith and reason, such as the evolution/ creation controversy, cognitive resonance is when ones beliefs fit well with science. If this occurs, then not only are we satisfied with the results we are also that much more confident in the discovery of truth.

The problem is that this particular issue is a controversy, which means cognitive dissonance is involved. Because the intellectual method of decision-making is superior in the search for truth about nature than the affective method, we must first alleviate cognitive dissonance by accommodating the new information by reconsidering our beliefs. We must invite examination of our beliefs and be open minded enough to change. In cases where Scripture meets nature, we must then seek resonance through dual revelation. The following are examples where examination through the dual revelation approach has identified flaws in anti-evolution claims.

## The Assyria Paradox

Geologists in the early 19th century took a serious look at the possibility of a recent global flood and concluded that there is absolutely no physical evidence for a major catastrophe of this magnitude. In 1961, Henry Morris and John Whitcomb, Jr. published *The Genesis Flood*, in which they claim to have resolved this Christian dilemma by arguing that scientists got it all wrong. They maintain that a global flood actually did occur in recent times and the physical evidence for this is all of the layered sedimentary rocks that blanket the continents. These rocks are cemented remnant global flood sediments. The study of this idea is called *modern flood geology*. Morris and Whitcomb founded what they call *creation science*, or the science of special creation, which is centered on modern flood geology. Geologists, on the other hand, have concluded that sedimentary rocks are the result of local depositional environments (beaches, deep sea muds, delta's, meandering rivers, *etc.*) followed by millions of years worth of burial, compaction, and cementation. In light of the dual revelation approach, flood geology must now be suspect. If we evaluate flood geology with a skeptical eye as we interpret Genesis, inconsistencies with it and the Bible become apparent. For example, accepting flood geology creates a biblical paradox. This paradox is caused by the mention of Assyria and the Tigris and Euphrates Rivers in Genesis 2: Modern young earth flood geology states that all of the layered sedimentary rocks around the world are remnant global flood sediment that has hardened into rock. These layered rocks can be seen when viewing the Grand Canyon. This leads to a biblical paradox in Genesis. The first time Assyria (land of the Assyrians) is mentioned in the Bible is in Genesis 2:14, where it is being used to orient the reader geographically as to where the Tigris River flows before it enters the Garden of Eden.

-"And the name of the third river is Hiddekel (Tigris): that is it which goeth toward the east of *Assyria*. And the fourth river is Euphrates. (KJV)"

The land of Assyria assumed its name because of its first inhabitants, the Assyrians. According to the Bible, this began with Asshur, grandson of Noah and son of Shem (Gen 10:22, 31 & Num 24:22,24 *KJV*). The name, Assyria, has its origins in the name, Asshur, which is a post-Noah population. Even today the Tigris River still flows through the ancient land of Assyria (now modern-day Iraq).

How can Assyria be mentioned in the Bible even before Assyrians existed and inhabited that particular land? The only logical conclusion is that this story is written for future post-Assyrian generations (like us) that know where the land of Assyria is. Generations that predate Assyria would have no idea where the Tigris flowed, while generations that postdate Assyria would understand.

Later verses in Genesis (11:28) support this anachronistic approach of geographically orienting future biblical readers. Abraham came from the land of Ur *of the Chaldees*. Abraham is said to have lived around 1900 BC, while the Chaldeans did not come into history for another 1000 years. Since Abraham predated the existence of the Chaldean civilization, the mention of them is used to give future readers an idea of where Ur is in the Middle East.

The problem for young earth creationists is that Genesis 2:14 creates an impossible situation. They claim that there was a global flood a few thousand years ago, and all of the layered sedimentary rocks that cover the Earth are its remnants. The mud, clay, and sand sediments settled to the bottom of global deluge, and then lithified (hardened) into the sedimentary rocks we see today. The problem is that the pre-flood Tigris and Euphrates Rivers are currently flowing ON TOP of 6,000 feet of supposed global flood sediments. If the creation scientists are correct, Tigris and Euphrates rivers should be underneath the global flood sediment. The flood is younger than the more ancient rivers.

To get by this problem, creation scientists claim that today's Tigris and Euphrates rivers are not the same rivers, but are merely named after the two famous ancient rivers mentioned in Genesis. The original rivers are buried under 6000 feet of rock-hard flood sediment.

On the surface this seems like a solution, but there is still the problem of Assyria. Assyria is a POST-flood civilization and is located on the surface of the Earth above the sedimentary rocks. In Genesis it is used as a geographic guide to mark the path of the *original* Tigris River. This is irrefutable biblical evidence that the ancient Tigris River mentioned in Genesis is the same river as today's Tigris River. This is also supported by the fact that, even today; the Tigris River continues to flow through the land that was once Assyria.

The only way around this conflict is to say that there was a PRE-flood Assyrian civilization separate from the post-flood Assyrian civilization. A claim like this is just an exercise in saving an erroneous argument. Genesis chapter 5 is a list of Adam's descendants all the way to Noah, and nowhere is there any mention of a pre-flood Asshur or Assyria. According to tradition, the author of Genesis is Moses, and he would have had first-hand knowledge of the post-flood Assyrians and the Tigris River flowing through their land. Why would he have mentioned the Tigris River flowing through Assyria in the second chapter of Genesis if there was a separate pre-flood Assyrian civilization coincidentally having a different Tigris River flowing through it? This would have caused his intended readers, Noah's descendents, to confuse the accuracy of God's word. Besides, this line of argument goes against Moses' pattern of using an anachronistic approach in orienting his readers, as evidenced by Abraham coming from Ur of the Chaldees.

The creators of the King James Thompson's Chain Reference Bible also agree that the Tigris River mentioned in Genesis 2:14 and today's Tigris River are one in the same. To the right of the Genesis 2:14 verse is the word, Assyria, and it is linked to Genesis 10:22, which refers to Asshur, the grandson of Noah. This means that an honest literal interpretation of the Book of Genesis cannot allow for the sedimentary rocks being the sedimentary remnants of Noah's flood.

The "fourth river Euphrates" also creates a biblical paradox if we accept flood geology. The Euphrates River mentioned in Genesis 2:14 should have been destroyed by Noah's flood, but it re-enters the biblical scene in the Book of Revelation:

-"Saying to the sixth angel which had the trumpet, Loose the four angels which are bound in the *great* river Euphrates." (Rev 9:14 KJV)
-"And the sixth angel poured out his vial upon the *great* river Euphrates; and the water thereof was dried up, that the way of the kings of the *east* might be prepared" (Rev 16:12 KJV)

The Euphrates River in these two verses is modified by the word, great, which strongly suggests that this river is one of the four special Garden of Eden Rivers. It makes sense that angels would reside in a river from the original Garden and not in a later namesake river. God even used angels (cherubim) and a divinely created flaming sword to guard the Garden and its rivers. Also, notice in Revelation 16:12 it states that the Euphrates River flowed in the east, since it blocked the kings of the east. Recall that Genesis 2:8 states Eden was located in the east.

-"And the LORD God planted a garden eastward in Eden; and there he put the man whom he had formed."

## The Nile Canyon and an Evaporating Mediterranean Sea

Scientists discovered massive concentrations of rock salt and gypsum at the bottom of the Mediterranean Sea. Even before this discovery, it was known that rock salt and gypsum are formed by evaporated seawater. What this discovery shows is that the Mediterranean Sea has evaporated completely a number of times in the past when it was blocked from being re-supplied with seawater by the Atlantic Ocean through the Gibraltar Straits. Massive broken up debris just inside the Mediterranean Sea indicates that once the Gibraltar Strait opened back up, a massive waterfall formed as the Mediterranean Sea was being refilled.

If we accept the global flood proponents' model, the Mediterranean Sea is a post-flood formation. So, when did it evaporate, and how long did the entire Mediterranean Sea take to evaporate? The Book of Genesis has a chronology beginning with Noah. Ancient Egypt has written history for the last 5,000 years. Nowhere is it mentioned about an evaporating Mediterranean Sea. Contemporaries to the ancient Egyptians were the Minoans. They were a sea faring society in the Mediterranean Sea. This culture would not have existed if the Mediterranean Sea had evaporated.

Then there is the problem of the Nile canyon. On either side of the Nile River are sedimentary rock layers, but the river itself is not sitting on top of these layers. The Nile River sits on top of a filled canyon buried by sand and silt sediment deposits. How did this canyon form? As the Mediterranean Sea was evaporating, the Nile River was carving out a canyon just like the Colorado River did to create the Grand Canyon. This is because of increased erosional forces at the mouth of the river as sea level lowered. The other major rivers emptying into the Mediterranean Sea also carved out canyons. The canyon walls are very steep, which suggests that the rivers carved through rocks instead of muds and sands. Just look at the low slope of a pile of dirt as compared to the high slope of the rock walls of the Grand Canyon and the Niagara Gorge. Loose sediment is never at a steep angle like a rock cliff. As the Mediterranean Sea began to fill up again, the canyon filled up with sands and silts through the normal process of river deposition.

According to Genesis 10:6, Egypt started out as a person. He was the grandson of Noah (son of Ham). Very soon after in Genesis 12:10 it states that Abraham brought his family to Egypt, the country, which already had a significant civilization ruled by Pharaohs. According to biblical chronology, Abraham was sixty years old when Noah died. This means that Noah's grandson, Egypt, formed a large civilization even before Noah's death. Since Noah was 600 years old at the time of the flood and 950 years old when he died, then a major population flourished in Egypt in just 350 years.

Where then, is the time available for the Mediterranean Sea to completely evaporate and cause the Nile River to cut a mile deep canyon, and then get filled up with sediment deposits so that Egypt and Minoa could begin to form large Mediterranean civilizations? Noah's grandson MUST have been alive during the time the evaporating Mediterranean Sea and the deep Nile River canyon. If so, why is there no record of this canyon in ancient Egyptian records? Even the most ancient of Egyptian cities lies on top of the filled Nile canyon.

The only way around the Nile Canyon paradox for global flood proponents is to say that the canyon was formed immediately after the flood. If the rock layers came from Noah's flood, then these lithified (formed into rock) sediment deposits are very close in age to the loose sediment deposits under the Nile River. The problem is that none of these sediments today show any hint of lithifying even though they are considered nearly as ancient as the rocks themselves. The rocks are fully sedimentary rocks, while the sediments are nothing but sediments. An ancient earth scenario explains that the rock layers and the sediment deposits are millions of years in age apart, which matches this physical evidence.

## The Niagara and St. David's Gorge

The Niagara Gorge is about eleven kilometers long, and has been created by Niagara Falls eroding the rocks underneath it. When it was flowing at full capacity, it was eroding the rocks at a rate of 3-6 feet per year. About 14,000 years ago Lake Erie and Lake Ontario were one huge lake; the product of the melting of a massive continental glacier. As the freshwater drained into the ocean, the water level lowered until it began flowing over the Niagara escarpment (a cliff) in between Lake Erie and Lake Ontario. This was the beginning of Niagara Falls, which occurred around 11,000 years ago, as confirmed by radiometric dating. The gorge has been getting larger ever since.

Some young earth creation scientists use the Niagara Gorge as supportive evidence of a young earth. Since Niagara Falls and Niagara Gorge began just thousands of years ago, this indicates when Noah's flood occurred followed by a short glacial period. These religiously motivated activists have failed to take into account St. David's Gorge. It is a buried gorge almost identical in size and shape to Niagara Gorge. The only difference is that it is completely buried in glacial sediment (till). It crosses the Niagara Gorge like an "X". Since it is buried with glacial till, it must have formed BEFORE the continental glacier arrived. The massive glacier then had to cover it in order to cause it to completely fill up with glacial sediment, such as gravel. This causes a bit of a problem for creation scientists. Their model suggests only a few hundred years between the great flood and the continental glacier. Is that enough time to gouge out an 11-kilometer gorge, and then completely fill it up with gravel?

Since the slope of the St. David's Gorge rock walls are identical to the walls in the Niagara Gorge, then the sediment layers that were gouged out creating the St. David's Gorge must have been rocks. The rate of formation of the Niagara Gorge took thousands of years to cut through the rocks, and the creation scientists support this claim. How could the St. David's Gorge have carved out an 11 kilometer gorge in less than one hundred years, yet have almost identical characteristics as the Niagara Gorge does? Gouging out a gorge in loose sediment is impossible. It would merely make a low sloping valley.

## Methuselah and Prometheus

According to a restrictive literal interpretation of the Book of Genesis, Noah's flood occurred around 2,250 BC to 2,350 BC. How is this known? The key is Abraham. We will follow the lead of Arch Bishop Ussher, who in 1658 determined that creation began in 4004 BC by adding up biblical dates and genealogies. Chapter 11 of Genesis is a genealogical list from Noah, the father of mankind, to Abraham, the father of the Israelites. It gives the name of each descendant, and when they fathered their successive son (put in parentheses): Noah (500 years), Shem (100), FLOOD (two years prior to the birth of Arpach'shad), Arpach'shad (35 years), Shelah (30), Eber (34), Peleg (30), Re'u (32), Serug (30), Nehor (29), Terah (70), and Abraham. Because of this, we know that Abraham was born 292 years after the flood, and lived for 175 years (Gen 25:7).

This also means that Abraham was 60 years old when Noah died, since Noah lived a further 350 years after the flood. Most Christian historians place Abraham at around 1900 BC. Genesis 9:29 states that Noah lived to 950 years, which puts Noah's birth at about 2,850 BC. Noah was 600 years old when the flood occurred, which places the date of the flood to about 2,250 BC, plus or minus a hundred years. (Gen 11:10)

This literal date for the flood is promoted by the Answers-in-Genesis young earth creationists in their article, *The Date of Noah's Flood*, written by John Osgood:

"Genesis 11:10 tells us that Shem was 100 years old, 2 years after the Flood had finished. When was Noah's Flood? 1,981 years to AD 0 plus 967 years to the founding of Solomon's Temple plus 480 years to the end of the Exodus plus 430 years to the promise to Abraham plus 75 years to Abraham's birth plus 350 years to Shem's 100th birthday plus 2 years to the Flood. The Biblical data places the Flood at 2304 BC +/- 11 years. (AIG)"

For the global flood proponents who claim that all of the world's sedimentary rocks are the remnants of Noah's flood, these biblical facts create a limit to how old any living creature can be. The oldest any living thing growing on top of sedimentary rocks can be is the age of the flood, or about 4,310 years (4,355 years according to Ussher).

According to the Great Basin National Park Service, Methuselah is the oldest bristlecone pine tree at 4735 years. Prometheus, at over 4,950 years, was the oldest bristlecone pine until a graduate student cut it down in 1964. The graduate student was taking core samples of bristlecone pines to determine their ages. His core sampler broke, so he received permission from the United States Forest Service to cut one of the bristlecone pines down. Soon after, they realized he cut down the oldest living thing on Earth. Because of this, bristlecone pines are protected, and Methuselah's location is a secret.

If the young earth creationists at Answers-in-Genesis are correct, then Methuselah and Prometheus were 480 years old and 695 years old, respectively, at the time of the global flood. If we accept their arguments for a recent global flood, then this creates a paradox. The bristlecone pines are growing ON TOP of the supposed global flood sediment. It seems an extreme stretch of logic to suggest that Methuselah, Prometheus, and their bristlecone pine cousins simultaneously separated from the ground as the flood approached, floated for one year together, then landed in their present location. Besides, God stated that ALL of life outside the ark perished (Genesis 6:17, 7:23). Methuselah and Prometheus should have died. Noah bringing the pines onboard and then traveling to America to replant them also seems highly unlikely.

To further complicate matters, older dead bristlecone pines found in the same location can be cross-matched with the living bristlecone pines by using their tree ring patterns. This technique is called dendrochronology, which has demonstrated that there has been a continuous residency time of these trees in this area for at least 9,000 years. Even older trees have been discovered, which may extend this time to well over 10,000 years. The tree ring ages have been confirmed by radiometric dating.

Global flood proponents are fond of accusing local flood proponents of compromising their beliefs in order to fit non-biblical facts, such as discoveries made in science. One way global flood proponents can attempt to get around the Methuselah and Prometheus paradox is to compromise with a restrictive literal biblical genealogy, the very same act in which they criticize local flood proponents of doing. For example, Morris and Whitcomb claim that the genealogy from Noah to Abraham must represent something other than a purely literal interpretation. They have compromised a purely literal interpretation because of irrefutable archaeological evidence. In *The Genesis Flood*, Morris and Whitcomb state,

"Near Eastern cultures apparently have a rather continuous archaeological record (based upon occupation levels and pottery chronology) back to at least the fifth millennium B.C., and it seems impossible to fit a catastrophe of the proportions depicted in Genesis 6-9 into such an archaeological framework."

They use this scientific evidence to support their belief that Genesis 11 is approximately 1,000 years longer than a purely restrictive literal interpretation. This particular statement of interpreting the Bible with scientific evidence contradicts Morris' earlier statement that it is "mandatory" to view scientific evidence in light of biblical evidence. They are playing both sides of the field. Also, the archaeological evidence that Morris and Whitcomb have compromised with actually shows a continuous record dating back to the eighth millennium BC, as in the case with the continuous settlement at Jericho. This seems to be too much of a stretch to harmonize with their favored literal interpretation, which may be why they published a fifth millennium BC date. Regardless, it still demonstrates a practice of compromise with science they claim is inappropriate. Young earth creationists such as Ken Ham at Answers-in-Genesis would argue against Morris and Whitcomb inadvertently using the dual revelation approach.

### Why Did God Hardwire Our Minds so Prone to Internal Conflict?

A perfectly appropriate question for a Christian to ask is why would God create our human minds with an emotional pathway that tends to hijack the intellectual pathway? One particular creationist response to this is that God did not create this imperfection. It was the result of original sin. Prior to the original sin, Adam and Eve possessed brains that were super-intelligent and incapable of cognitive dissonance. This argument can be extrapolated from their argument as to why Adam could name thousands of animals in just one day. Young earth creationist Russell Grigg, writes in his answersingenesis. org article, *Naming the Animals: All in a Day's Work for Adam,*

"...man's mental powers, reason, and capacity for articulate, grammatical, symbolic speech. In Adam, before sin, these capacities may have dwarfed anything we know today."

I have always had a difficult time with this kind of argument. First, nowhere in the Bible does it say that original sin caused man to become less intelligent than Adam and Eve. Second, this explanation conflicts with even a restrictive literal interpretation of Genesis. The serpent easily bamboozled Eve into eating the fruit and Eve easily convinced Adam to betray God's commandment. Would super-humans make these mistakes? They certainly seem awfully human to me.

I am not going to claim to understand why God created our minds this way, but if we look at it from an evolutionary perspective and with physical evidence, we may get closer to the truth. Recall Dr. Simón explained that the use of the emotional pathway is the more primitive cognitive process as compared to the intellectual pathway. As human beings evolved, the cerebral cortex became more involved with decision-making. Our brains are a result of biological evolution and common ancestry. From a Christian perspective, this is *how* God created us, and we have inherited our ancestral past. Original sin had nothing to do with why we are prone to internal conflict, nature did.

I suspect the reason why God created us through a natural process has something to do with free will. Free will is the ability to make a decision, regardless if it is right or wrong, or good or bad. Having a limbic system for emotions and a cerebral cortex for reason gives us a wide variety of decisions to freely choose from, not just the correct one. God could have created us perfect and incapable of sin. If this had occurred, then we would not have had the ability to choose anything but the correct decision, specifically, to choose to love God. We would not have had free will. Is it not better to have someone love you on their own volition as opposed to forcing them to love you? Once God introduced the randomness factor into nature, free will became a reality. *Free will is not only a gift to us; it is a gift to God.* God can now be loved just as we are.

# Bibliography

Anzai, T., Shiina, T., Kimura, N., Yanagiya, K., Kohara, S., Shigenari, A., Yamagata, T., Kulski, J., Naruse, T., Fujimori, Y., Fukuzumi, Y. Yamazaki, M., Tashiro, H., Iwamoto, C., Umehara, Y., Imanishi, T., Meyer, A., Ikeo, K., Gojobori, T., Bahram, S., & Inoko, H., (2003). *Comparative sequencing of human and chimpanzee MHC Class I regions unveils insertions/deletions as the major path to genomi c divergence.* Proc Natl Acad Sci USA 100(13), 7708-7713.

Aquinas, T. (1273). *Summa Theologiae* [Summary of Theology]. (Christian Classics Ethereal Library, Calvin College, Grand Rapids, MI) http://www.ccel.org/ccel/ aquinas/summa.html.

Ammerman, N. T. *Baptist Battles: Social Change and Religious Conflict in the Southern Baptist Convention.* (New Brunswick : Rutgers University Press, 1990).

Archer, G. L. *Encyclopedia of Bible Difficulties.* (Zondervan, Grand Rapids, MI, 2001).

Ashcraft, C. (2004). *Genetic Variability by Design.* TJ 18(2).

Augustine (408). *On the Literal Meaning of Genesis*, trans. John Hammond Taylor, S. J. *Ancient Christian Writers.* 41 (Newman Press, 1982).

Axelrod, R. (1973). *Schema theory: an information processing model of perception and cognition.* The American Political Science Review, 67, 1248-1266.

Baigent, M., Leigh, R., & Lincoln, H. *The Holy Blood and the Holy Grail.* (Bantam Dell Publishing, New York, 1982).

Bartelt, K. (1998). *A Visit to the Institute for Creation Research.* (The Talk.Origins Archive Website, Houston, Texas). http://talkorigins.org.

Battle, J. A. (1997). *Charles Hodge, Inspiration, Textual Criticism, and the Princeton Doctrine of Scripture.* WRS Journal (4/2), 28-44.

Baylor Institute for Studies of Religion. (September 2006). *American Piety in the 21st Century.* (Baylor University, Waco, Texas). http://www.baylor.edu/content/ services/ document.php/33304.pdf.

Bebbington, D. W. *The Dominance of Evangelicalism: The Age of Spurgeon and Moody* (InterVarsity, 2005).

Bechara, A., Damasio, H., Damasio, A.R., & Lee, G.P., (1999). *Different Contributions of the Human Amygdala and Ventromedial Prefrontal Cortex to Decision-making.* Journal of Neuroscience, 19(13), 5473-81.

Beckett, E., Bernitt, H., & Chandra, V. (1998). *Sun Gods.* (Oracle Education Foundation, Redwood Shores, CA, 1998). http://library.thinkquest.org/15215/ Culture/Sun_gods.html.

Beeman, W. O. *Fighting the good fight: fundamentalism and religious revival.* J. MacClancy, el. Anthropology for the Real World, (University of Chicago Press, Chicago, Illinois, 2001).

Britain, T. (1999). *Just What Do They Say, Dr. Morris?* Reports of the National Center for Science Education (RNCSE), 19(1), 22-23.

Brown, T. *Peer Review and the Acceptance of New Scientific Ideas.* (Sense About Science, London, 2004).

Brown, W. *In the Beginning: Compelling Evidence for Creation and the Flood* (6th ed). (Center for Scientific Creation, Phoenix, AR, 1996).

Carroll, R. L. *Pattern and Processes of Vertebrate Evolution.* (Cambridge U Press, New York, 1997).

Carroll, R. T. (2006). *Confirmation Bias.* (The Skeptics Dictionary, 1994-2007). http://skepdic.com/confirmbias.html.

Cherry, S. *Crisis management via Biblical Interpretation: Fundamentalism, Modern Orthodoxy, and Genesis.* In *Jewish Tradition and Challenge of Darwinism,* editors Cantor, G. & Swetlitz M. (University of Chicago Press, 2006).

Colby, C. (1996). *Introduction to Evolutionary Biology.* (The Talk.Origins Archive Website, Houston, Texas). http://talkorigins.org.

Cramer, R. N. (2004). *The King James Version and the Textus Receptus.* (BibleTexts. com website). http://www.bibletexts.com.

Crawford, H. *Sumer and the Sumerians.* (Cambridge Univ. Press, 1991).

Curtis, H., & Barnes, N. S. *Biology* (5th ed.). (Worth Publishers, 1989).

Damasio, A. R. (1994). *Descartes' Error: Emotion, Reason, and the Human Brain.* (New York; G.P. Putnam).

Darwin, C. *On the Origin of Species by Means of Natural Selection, or the Preservation of Favoured Races in the Struggle for Life.* (John Murry, London, 1859).

Digitale, E. (2005). *Conferring with the Dalai Lama.* Spotlight. (The Regents of the University of California, Davis campus). http://www.ucdavis.edu/spotlight/0505/dalai_lama.html.

Durbin, P. G. *Beware of False Memories in Regressive Hypnotherapy.* (The Alchemy Institute of Healing Arts, Santa Rosa, California, 1999-2006). www.alchemyinstitute.com/false-memory.html.

Elliott, M. (2005). *The Fundamentals, Higher Criticism and Archaeology.* (Bible and Interpretation, Cheyenne, WY). http://www.bibleinterp.com/articles/ Elliott_Fundamentals.htm.

Elsberry, W. R. *The "Wedge" Document.* (AntiEvolution.org, 2001). http://www.antievolution.org/features/wedge.html.

Festinger, L. *A theory of cognitive dissonance.* (Stanford, CA: Stanford University Press, 1957).

Forrest, B. *Intelligent Design Creationism and its Critics.* (MIT Press, 2001).

Fuller O. (1970). *Is The King James Version Nearest To The Original Autographs?* (Tabernacle Baptist Church, Lubbock, Texas).

Futuyma, D. J. *Evolutionary Biology* (3$^{rd}$ ed.). (Sinauer Associates Inc, Sunderland, MA, 1998).

Gerard, J. (1909). *Galileo Galilei.* In The Catholic Encyclopedia. New York: Robert Appleton Company.

Geisler, N. *Baker Encyclopedia of Christian Apologetics.* (Baker Books, Grand Rapids, MI, 1999).

Giere R. N. *Understanding Scientific Reasoning.* (CBS College Publishing, New York, 2005 Edition).

Gish, D. *Evolution: The Fossils Say No!* (Creation-Life Publishers, San Diego, CA, 1978).

Gish, D. *Evolution: The Fossils Still Say No!* (Institute for Creation Research, El Cajon, CA, 1995).

Gould, S. J. *Ever Since Darwin* (5$^{th}$ ed.). (W. W. Norton & Company, New York, 1977).

Gould, S. J. *Hen's Teeth and Horse's Toes: Further Reflections in Natural History.* (W. W. Norton & Company, New York, 1983).

Gould, S. J. *The Flamingo's Smile.* (W. W. Norton & Company, New York, 1987).

Gould, S. J. *Eight Little Piggies.* (W. W. Norton & Company, New York, 1993).

Great Basin National Park Service (2002). *The "Prometheus" Story.* (National Park Service, U.S. Department of the Interior). http://www.nps.gov/archive/grba/Bristlecone%20Pines/bristleconepineprometheus.htm.

Grigg, R. M. (1995). *Did Darwin Recant?* Creation 18(1), 36-37.

Grigg, R. M. (1996). *Naming the Animals: All in a Day's Work for Adam.* Creation 18(4), 46-49.

Ham, K. (2004). *Jesus wrote all of the Bible!* Answers Update-US. (answersingenesis.org).

Hammack, L. (2006). *DNA confirms guilt.* The Roanoke Times, Roanoke, VA, Jan 13, 2006.

Hawley, M. L. (2001). *Fossil Faunal Distribution, Microstratigraphy, and Correlation of the Kashong Member: Sea Level Cycles and Westward Beveling in the Appalachian Foreland Basin.* (Masters Thesis Project, Buffalo State College, Buffalo, NY).

Heise, J. (1995). *The Akkadian Language.* (Netherlands Institute for Space Research, Netherlands) http://www.sron.nl/~jheise/akkadian/.

Heyrman, C. L. (2000). *The Church of England in Early America.* (National Humanities Center, Research Triangle Park, NC, 2007). http://nationalhumanitiescenter.org/tserve/ eighteen/ekeyinfo/chureng.htm.

Heyrman, C. L. (2000). *The First Great Awakening.* (National Humanities Center, Research Triangle Park, NC, 2007). http://nationalhumanitiescenter.org/tserve/ eighteen/ekeyinfo/grawaken.htm.

Heyrman, C. L. (2000). *Puritanism and Predestination.* (National Humanities Center, Research Triangle Park, NC, 2007). http://nationalhumanitiescenter.org/tserve/ eighteen/ekeyinfo/puritan.htm.

Holton, G., & Brush, S. G. *Physics, The Human Adventure - From Copernicus to Einstein and Beyond.* (Rutgers University Press, New Brunswick, NJ, & London, 2001).

Hsü, Kenneth J. *The Mediterranean Was a Desert.* (Princeton University Press, New Jersey, 1983).

ICL. (1978). *The Chicago Statement on Biblical Inerrancy.* (Internet Christian Library, Worldstar Internet Technologies). http://www.iclnet.org/pub/resources/ text/history/ chicago.stm.txt.

Isachsen, Y. W., Landing, E., Lauber, J. M., Rickard, L. V., & Rogers, W. B. *Geology of New York, A Simplified Account.* (The University of the State of New York, The State Education Department, Albany, NY, 1991).

Johnson, G. R. *Beyond Gap Theory Interpretation of Genesis.* (Christian Geology Ministry, 1997-2007). http://www.kjvbible.org/gap_theory.html.

Junqué, C. (1994). *El lóbulo frontal y sus disfunciones (The frontal lobe and its dysfunctions).* Neuropsicología (pp. 349-399). Madrid: Síntesis.

Kim, S., Elango, N., Warden, C., Vigoda, E., & Yi, S. (2006). *Heterogeneous Genomic Molecular Clocks in Primates.* PloS Genetics, 2(10).

Knox, E. (2004). *Luther.* (Boise State University). http://history.boisestate.edu/ westciv/.

Kuban, G. J. (1997). *Sea Monster or Shark? An Analysis of a Supposed Plesiosaur Carcass Netted in 1977.* (Reports of the National Center for Science Education, Oakland, CA, 17(3), 16-28).

Larson, E. J. *Summer for the Gods: The Scopes Trial and America's Continuing Debate over Science and Religion.* (Harvard University Press, 1998).

Lee, K. C., Chung, N., & Kim, J. S. (2004). *Analysis of Decision-Making Performance from a Schema Approach to Cognitive Resonance. Decision Support in an Uncertain and Complex world*: The IFIP TC8/WG8.3 International Conference.

Lubenow, M. *Bones of Contention.* (Baker Book House Co., Grand Rapids, MI, 1992).

Luther, Martin. *Vorrede zu Band I der Opera Latina der Wittenberger Ausgabe.* (6th ed.). (Berlin, 1545). Translated by Bro. Andrew Thornton, OSB.

Mahon, J. *A Little Logic.* (Washington and Lee University, Lexington, Virginia, 2007). http://home.wlu.edu/~mahonj/LittleLogic.htm.

Martin, G.C. *Olea europeas L. (Olive).* (U.S. Department of Agriculture Forestry Service, National Tree Seed Laboratory, Dry Branch, Georgia, 2007).

Martin, T. *Beyond Creation Science* (2nd Ed.). (Covenant Community Church, Whitehall, MT, 2005).

Martino, B., Kumaran, D., Seymour, B., & Dolan, R. (2006). *Frames, Biases, and Rational Decision-Making in the Human Brain.* Science, 313, 684-687.

Mason, S. F. *A History of the Sciences* (10th ed.). (Macmillan Publishing Co., Inc. New York, 1972).

Metzger, B. M. *A Textual Commentary of the Greek New Testament* (2nd ed.). (Sturrgart, 1993).

Miller, L. *Dendrochronology.* (Information received from Henri Grissino-Mayer of Laboratory Tree-Ring Research, Arizona Board of Regents, University of Arizona, Arizona, 2005). http://sonic.net/bristlecone/home.html.

Moran, L. A. (1993). *What is Evolution?* (Evolution by Accident Website, Toronto ON, Canada). http://bioinfo.med.utoronto.ca/Evolution_by_Accident/ What_Is_ Evolution.html.

Morris, H. *History of Modern Creationism.* (Masters Books, San Diego, CA, 1984).

Morris, J. *Tracking Those Incredible Dinosaurs and the People Who Knew Them.* (Bethany House Pub, Bloomington, Minnesota, 1982).

Morton, G. R. *Foundation, Fall, and Flood.* (DMD Publications, 1999 3rd edition).

Morton, G. R. (2003). *Why I Believe Genesis is Historically Accurate.* (DMD Publishing Company, Spring, Texas). http://home.entouch.net/dmd/genesis.htm.

National Academy of Sciences (NAS). *Science and Creationism: A View from the National Academy of Sciences.* (National Academy Press, 1999).

National Center for Science Education (NCSE). (2007). *Statements of Religious Organizations.* (National Center for Science Education, Oakland, CA). http:// www.ncseweb.org/resources/articles/7445_statements_from_religious_ org_12_19_2002.asp.

New York State Office of Court Administration. (2004). *Falsus in uno.* (New York State Criminal Jury Instruction 7.06 at 276, 2004).

Nissen, H. J., *The early history of the Ancient Near East, 9000-2000BC.* (University of Chicago Press, Chicago, London, 1988).

Numbers R. L. *The Creationists: From Scientific Creationism to Intelligent Design, expanded edition.* (Cambridge, MA, and London, England, 2006). ISBN-10: 0-674-02339-0. http://www.hup.harvard.edu/pdf/NUMCRX_excerpt.pdf.

Numbers R. L. *The Creationists: The Evolution of Scientific Creationism.* (University of California Press, 1992).

Numbers R. L. *The Disappointed: Millerism and Millenarianism in the Nineteenth Century.* (University of Tennessee Press, 1993).

Ohio History Central. (2005). *Social Gospel Movement.* (Ohio History Central Online Encyclopedia, Ohio). http://www.ohiohistorycentral.org/entry.php?rec=1527.

Ohta. Y, & Nishikimi, M. (1999). *Random nucleotide substitutions in primate nonfunctional gene for L-gulono-gamma-lactone oxidase, the missing enzyme in L-ascorbic acid biosynthesis.* Biochim Biophys Acta 1472:408-11. PubMed ID: 10572964.

Olson, C.E., & Miesel, S. *The Da Vinci Hoax.* (Ignatius Press, San Francisco, 2004).

Osgood, J. (1981). *The Date of Noah's Flood.* Creation 4(1):10-13.

Piaget, J. (1985). *The Equilibration of Cognitive Structures: The Central Problem of Intellectual Development.* Chicago: University of Chicago Press.

Rabbinical Council of America (RCA). (2005). *Creation, Evolution, and Intelligent Design.* (View of the Rabbinical Council of America, 2008). http://www.rabbis. org/news/ article.cfm?id=100635.

Raine, S. (2005). *Reconceptualising the human body: Heaven's Gate and the quest for divine transformation.* Religion 35(2), 98-117.

Riggins, R. (2002). *Do You Believe in Evolution?* (SkepticReport.com, 2002-2007). http://www.skepticreport.com/creationnism/believeevolution.htm.

Rumney, G. (2003). *Creationism? Good Grief!* (Otagosh.tripod.com, New Zealand, 2007). http://otagosh.tripod.com/creationism.pdf.

Sagan, C. *Cosmos.* (Random House, Inc., New York, 2002 Edition).

Sagan, C. *The Demon-Haunted World.* (Random House, Inc., New York, 1999).

Sawaf, T., Al-Saad, D., Gebran, A., Barazangi, M., Best, J., & Chaimove, T. (1993). *Stratigraphy and structure of Eastern Syria across the Euphrates depression.* Tectonophysics. 220, 267-281.

Schafersman, S. D. (1994). *An Introduction to Science, Scientific Thinking and the Scientific Method* (The Free Inquiry Website, Houston, Texas). www.freeinquiry. com/ intro-to-sci.html.

Schneider, R. J. *Does the Bible Teach Science?* (Berea College, Kentucky, 2005-2007). http://community.berea.edu/scienceandfaith/essay03.asp.

Scott, D. (2000). *Evangelicalism as a Social Movement.* (National Humanities Center, Research Triangle Park, NC, 2007). http://nationalhumanitiescenter.org/ tserve/ nineteen/nkeyinfo/nevansoc.htm.

Scott, D. (2000). *Evangelicalism, Revivalism, and the Second Great Awakening.* (National Humanities Center, Research Triangle Park, NC, 2007). http:// nationalhumanitiescenter.org/tserve/ nineteen/nkeyinfo/nevanrev.htm.

Semeniuk, I. (2007). *How Sputnik Changed the World.* New Scientist. 2620, 40-42.

Sexton, J. (2006). *NT Text Criticism and Inerrancy.* TMSJ. 17/1, 51-59.

Simanek, D. E. (2006). *The Flat Earth.* (Lock Haven University, Pennsylvania). http://www.lhup.edu/~dsimanek/flat/flateart.htm.

Simón, V. M. (1997). *Emotional Participation in Decision-Making.* Psicothema, 9, 365-376.

Sire, J.W. *The Universe Next Door: A Basic World view Catalog*

Sparks, R. J. (2003). *Religion in Mississippi.* Heritage of Mississippi Series, number 2. (Jackson: University Press of Mississippi, for the Mississippi Historical Society, Jackson. 2001).

Stoner, D. A. *New Look at an Old Earth; Resolving the Conflict Between the Bible and Science.* (Harvest House Publishers, Eugene, OR, 1997).

Tigay, J. H. (1987). *Genesis, Science, and "Scientific Creationism".* Conservative Judaism, 40(2), 20-27.

Tutsch, C. (2003). *Interpreting White's Earth History Statements with Particular Reference to the Genesis Flood.* (Ellen G. White Estate, Inc., Faith and Science Conference II, Glacier View, CO).

Valkenburgh, S. *A Dramatic Revival: The First Great Awakening in Connecticut.* 1996 Ralph Waldo Emerson Prize. (The Concord Review, Inc., Sudbury, MA, 1995).

Wacker, G. (2000). *The Rise of Fundamentalism.* (National Humanities Center, Research Triangle Park, NC, 2007). http://nationalhumanitiescenter.org/tserve/ twenty/tkeyinfo/ fundam.htm.

Wagar, B., & Thagard, P. (2004). *Spiking Phineas Gage: A Neurocomputational Theory of Cognitive-Affective Integration in Decision Making.* Psychological Review, 111, 67-79.

Wagner, S. *The Mysterious Ica Stones*. (About.com: Paranormal Phenomena, New York Times Co, 2007). http://paranormal.about.com/cs/ancientanomalies/a/aa041904.htm.

Wells, S. *The Journey of Man: A Genetic Odyssey*. (Princeton University Press, 2003).

Whitcomb, J. C., & Morris, H. M. *The Genesis Flood*. (Presbyterian & Reformed Publishing, New Jersey, 1960).

Whitefield, R. (2001). *Reading Genesis One*. (Rodney Whitefield Publisher, San Jose, CA).

Wikipedia. (2007). *History of Creationism*. (Wikimedia Foundation). http://en.wikipedia.org/wiki/History_of_creationism.

Winchester, S. *The Map That Changed the World*. (HarperCollins Publishers Inc., New York, 2001).

Young, D. A. (1988). *The contemporary Relevance of Augustine's View of Creation*. Perspectives on Science and Christian Faith, 40/1:42-45.

Breinigsville, PA USA
24 October 2010
247925BV00004B/7/P